In memory of William Fitzhugh Murrah
Library Board of Trustees, January 1955 - May 1977
Library Board President, December 1969 - May 1977

Given by Paul Preston & Corinne Murrah Wilson

THE DAY THE WAR BEGAN

THE DAY THE WAR BEGAN

ARCHIE SATTERFIELD

PRAEGER

Westport, Connecticut
London

Copyright Acknowledgments

The author and publisher gratefully acknowledge permission to use the following copyrighted sources.

Wenkham, Robert. *Honolulu Is an Island.* Chicago: Rand McNally, 1978. Reprinted with permission.

Days of '41—Pearl Harbor Remembered by Ed Sheehan, published by Honolulu Branch 46, Fleet Reserve Association Enterprises, P.O. Box 6067, Honolulu, Hawaii 96818. Reprinted with permission.

Library of Congress Cataloging-in-Publication Data

Satterfield, Archie.
The day the war began / Archie Satterfield.
p. cm.
Includes bibliographical references and index.
ISBN 0-275-94251-1 (alk. paper)
1. Pearl Harbor (Hawaii), Attack on, 1941. 2. World War, 1939–1945—Causes. 3. World War, 1939–1945—United States.
I. Title.
D767.92.S35 1992
940.54'26—dc20 92-3364

British Library Cataloguing in Publication Data is available.

Library of Congress Catalog Card Number: 92-3364
ISBN: 0-275-94251-1

First published in 1992

Praeger Publishers, 88 Post Road West, Westport, CT 06881
An imprint of Greenwood Publishing Group, Inc.

Printed in the United States of America

The paper used in this book complies with the Permanent Paper Standard issued by the National Information Standards Organization (Z39.48-1984).

10 9 8 7 6 5 4 3 2 1

Dedicated to my classmates of the West Plains, Missouri, high school class of 1951: Children of the Great Depression and World War II, we came of age while America was at its peak.

Contents

	Introduction: Saturday, December 6, 1941	1
1	The First Shot	21
2	The Americans Fight Back	27
3	Adventures of the *Henley*	43
4	Game Called Due to War	49
5	View from the Cane Fields	53
6	Friendly Fire	61
7	A Chinese-American Family	66
8	Hell on a Sunshiny Day	70
9	The Military Takes Over Hawaii	77
10	Niihau Fights Back	82
11	The Saga of the *Pacific Clipper*	86
12	The Forgotten Attack	93
13	On the Home Front	97
14	War Comes to the Football Game	105
15	The Delayed Message	114

16	The White House Prepares for War	120
17	War Becomes a Reality	124
18	Extra! Extra!	132
19	Strange New Words	135
20	Sudden Heroes	142
21	The Mating Dance Continues	149
22	The Nation Unifies	154
23	Hawaii's Longest Night	157
24	Defending the East Coast	162
25	"I Slept Like a Baby"	166
	Bibliography	169
	Index	173

THE DAY THE WAR BEGAN

Introduction: Saturday, December 6, 1941

Christmas was in the air on Saturday, December 6, 1941, and the chill of early winter was felt across most of America, even in New Orleans, where a cold wind blew off the Mississippi River delta. It had been two weeks since Thanksgiving, Christmas was not quite three weeks away, shoppers were out in record numbers in most cities, and merchants were predicting the best Christmas shopping season since 1928. Some cities had extra police on the streets to control traffic, something that had not been needed in previous years.

Most Americans felt more secure than at any time during the past decade. Jobs were available again, and new factories were being built all across the country to arm Britain, France, and China. Soldiers and sailors had been going through the most intensive training since World War I, but most maneuvers would soon be suspended so the men could go home for the holidays. Talk of war was in the newspapers and on the radio; but this was America, and hardly anyone felt directly threatened. Most people went about their lives with no sense of urgency.

One of those Americans going about his life with a sense of purpose and accomplishment was John J. Slattery, a member of the research team that developed the first Army Radio Position Finding system to protect America against attack by enemy planes. Soon the system would be known universally as "radar," a word coined by the Navy, but in 1941 it was still shrouded in secrecy while England and America raced against the Germans to develop the best such system.

For months Slattery and his team had been working long hours at the Army Signal Corps laboratories in Fort Monmouth, New Jersey. They did so with a sense of urgency as the war in Europe worsened and the verbal war with Japan intensified. The system had already proven itself for England during the Battle of Britain. Although Slattery was tired on the weekend of December 6–7, 1941, he and his fellow engineers felt a great sense of accomplishment. The equipment they designed had been working as well as they dared hope. Several sets had been installed: along both American coasts, in the American territories of Hawaii and the Philippines, at the entrances to the Panama Canal, and in Iceland. Now Slattery was home for a quiet weekend with his wife and their fourteen-month-old son.

"The reports on the equipment were very good, and we were elated," Slattery said. "However, there was a general unease about the diplomatic exchanges of our State Department and the Japanese emissaries. Those of us who were active in military research and development felt that a crisis was at hand but had no specific idea how it might evolve."

Although radar had already proven its value in the Battle of Britain, the American military leaders did not yet take it very seriously. In Hawaii and the Philippines the stations were operated only sporadically, even though war warnings had been issued from Washington to these isolated American outposts.

In Louisville, Kentucky, a public relations counselor and newspaperman named Henry S. Evans had his own fears. All during the 1930s and into the 1940s, he had been convinced that Japan was preparing to conquer the United States. Japan was doing so by buying the weapons—steel, scrap iron, entire mills, and the technology to make its own steel—from the United States. Evans believed all of this would be used against the United States in the war he was certain would come. Evans was not a lone voice in the wilderness of those Great Depression years, but the message he had been delivering through various media had not been heeded. On that Saturday he was positive war with Japan was inevitable and would come soon. The only thing he did not know was when or where the opening shots would be fired.

America's Pacific Fleet, more than a hundred vessels strong, was in Pearl Harbor for the weekend. Part of the fleet had been on training exercises during the past week; and the two carriers, the *Enterprise* and the *Lexington,* were still at sea with their destroyer and cruiser escorts, delivering fighters to the Marines on Wake and Midway islands. Both carriers were due back on the weekend. Otherwise, the fleet was in as usual, lined up neatly at mooring buoys around Ford Island and along the piers of the shipyard. Two-thirds of the crewmen were ashore on liberty.

Torpedoman Third Class Don Wilson, a Kansas boy who was a member of the original crew that went aboard the destroyer *Henley* in 1938 shortly after she was commissioned, was on duty that weekend. Just after dark Saturday evening he was sent over to Ford Island in the ship's launch for the guard mail, the official mail that included all orders. He wore his dress white uniform and carried a .45-caliber automatic pistol. As the boat went through the maze of vessels, he could see movies playing on the fantails of the battleships lined up along the island. Wilson did not stay up late that night because he had to get up early the next morning to help install warheads on torpedoes. With the new warnings from Washington, the Navy decided it would be a good idea to have all fighting ships prepared. So when the *Henley* came in from escorting battleships, her fuel tanks were topped off, ammunition stores were checked and filled, and the dummy heads on the torpedoes were replaced with explosive warheads.

The average American thought of war occasionally, but war was a remote prospect almost completely detached from the reality of American life. Few people thought about the situation in the Pacific at all, and only a handful of Americans knew or cared that the Japanese fleet was at large somewhere in the Pacific beyond the scrutiny of America and her allies. All of these nations were convinced Japan was going to attack in a matter of days, and each hoped the attack would be against one of the others.

Most Americans did not feel threatened, and except for those with men in the military service it seemed too remote to contemplate. Most believed that their lives were gradually improving and the darkness of the 1930s was lifting. Many of the millions of families who were victims of the stock market crash of 1929 and the droughts that had hit in 1934, 1936, and 1939, had been migratory for as long as a decade. Now they were finding places to work and to live, and many were returning to the Midwest from which they had fled when the wind blew away the topsoil, creating the Dust Bowl and causing thousands of farms in the Great Plains to be abandoned.

The Dust Bowl came in the middle of the Great Depression; these catastrophic events were compounded by the emergence of mechanized farming. Marginal farmers and farm workers had no chance. The Okies (a derisive name for anyone on the road and without a home) began wandering from the Midwest, the South, and the Great Plains in search of work and another permanent home. It was the greatest movement of people in America since the Oregon Trail migrations of the early years of the nineteenth century. There was one major difference, however: These migrants had no free land waiting for them at the end of the trail.

Mechanization is the major factor often overlooked in this displacement of rural dwellers. Indeed, had the droughts not occurred, many of the migrants would have been on the road anyway. For example, in the southern states the number of tractors increased from around 30,000 in 1930 to 100,000 in 1938. During this same period the mechanical cotton picker was introduced, having an enormous impact on the 40,000 cotton pickers who traveled up to 1,000 miles each season, following the crop. Other farm workers did not specialize but worked in the fields or orchards where crops needed to be harvested by hand—lettuce, cotton, peas, potatoes, beets, and citrus fruits. In 1934 nearly 400,000 individuals and 16,000 families were registered with the Federal Emergency Relief Administration as transients, and between 1935 and 1939 more than 350,000 were registered entering California.

During the 1930s the nation's population had increased by 8 million, to a total of 131 million by 1940. The increase was only 7 percent, compared with a 16 percent increase during the previous decade. The major factors in this population slowdown were limits on immigration, later marriages, more women in the work force, an increasing knowledge and use of birth control, and a reluctance among couples to have large families during such an economically lean period. One statistical report on the period blamed "the deterrent biological influence of an urban environment" for the low birth rate, although history does not support this statement.

The Farm Security Administration photographers, who were to record the 1930s better than any period in American history has been recorded, were still working in the field and were beginning to branch out to American territories: When the war came, at least one photographer was in Puerto Rico, documenting farming conditions there. It is to them that we owe our lasting visual symbols of the 1930s: The collection of photographs of the rural regions of America constitute an icon of the era. No matter how pleasant life might have been for many people—and it was very pleasant for many Americans during that period, because not everyone was desperately poor—we shall always think of those prewar years as grim, gray, and gritty because that is the way the official photographs of the era portrayed America.

The American economy was steadily improving when the winter of 1941–42 arrived. Although more than 4 million men were out of work—boxcars were a necessary means of transportation for millions and hobo jungles their housing projects—the Great Depression had already been replaced by the wartime economy. At the height of the Depression in 1933, more than fourteen million were unemployed; in the middle of the war, unemployment remained at about four million, what it had been in December 1941. Job listings in newspapers had steadily increased as the defense industry supplied our European allies and China with field weapons, airplanes, armored vehicles, and ships—in November alone thirty-three warships had been launched. By 1941 prosperity no longer seemed unattainable. The jobless were finding work again. Things were picking up. New automobiles, one of the best indicators of economic health, were rolling off the assembly lines in greater numbers; the best-selling car that year was the Chevrolet, with 930,000 sold at an average price of $700. The Great Depression was over.

By the end of 1941 Americans not only were doing well financially; our personal health was improving on a national basis. Women's magazines, government programs, better education for schoolteachers, and the efforts of food companies helped create a national awareness of good nutrition. An immediate result noted in 1942 was that the average American soldier was five pounds heavier and an inch taller than his predecessors in World War I, some twenty-five years earlier.

New medical breakthroughs were coming regularly, the latest being the announcement in the December 3 issue of the *Journal of the American Medical Association* that the American medical community had accepted Elizabeth Kenny's method of treating polio victims. The Australian nurse had been treating polio among Aborigines by massaging the affected muscles, moving them, and in general reeducating the muscles.

The worldwide military buildup was reflected in many aspects of American life, including new products and new technology presented in technical magazines. The old standby, *Popular Mechanics,* was laden with military hardware and gadgetry. The September 1941 issue carried an article about a blackout lamp for automobiles, a one-candlepower light that enabled drivers to see street signs. Another article described the military vehicles developed for Uncle Sam. These included motorcycles for machine gunners, trackless tanks, jeeps (which the magazine accurately predicted would replace motorcycles), and bulletproof tires.

Some of Hollywood's best films were made between 1938 and 1941. The critics' favorite 1941 film was Orson Welles's *Citizen Kane,* still considered by many to be the best film ever made. In spite of its popularity with the critics, on December 7, 1941, it was showing in only a few theaters across the country because the model for Kane, newspaper magnate William Randolph Hearst, waged a campaign against its being shown.

The most popular films in 1941 were lighthearted comedies and an occasional war movie. In the former category were *Sun Valley Serenade* with Sonja Henie and John Payne, *Appointment for Love* with Charles Boyer and Margaret Sullavan, and *Caught in the Draft* with Bob Hope and Dorothy Lamour.

In the war category were *Dive Bomber* with Fred MacMurray and Errol Flynn and *Sergeant York* with Gary Cooper and Joan Leslie. The latter was one of the year's most popular films, and would become more so after December 7.

We did not realize it at the time, but we were experiencing radio's golden age. Radio had a wide variety of programs then and did not have to compete with television. We listened to some of the most imaginative comedy ever performed. Very seldom did the humor sting, and when a comedian fired a broadside at someone, it was usually one of his friends who could shoot back with the same comedic skills. Some of the most famous feuds involved Edgar Bergen and his group of dummies—Charlie McCarthy and Mortimer Snerd, and later Effie Klinker and Podine Puffington. Bergen and his dummies represented the only instance when a ventriloquist did not have to be seen to be appreciated. Their identities were so well defined that once we had seen a photograph of Bergen with his sharp nose and bemused smile, and Charlie with his tuxedo and monocle, we never needed to see them again to imagine what they looked like in front of the microphones.

Charlie was the smart-mouthed dummy and Mortimer the stupid one. Charlie, to Bergen's horror and embarrassment, took on all the wits of the day. He and W. C. Fields were wonderful together, with Fields calling Charlie "the little woodpecker's snack bar," and Charlie telling the hard-drinking Fields that "Pink elephants take aspirin to get rid of W. C. Fields."

Perhaps the greatest of the feuds was between two close friends, Fred Allen and Jack Benny, who were distinguished among comedians for their common decency. Their exchanges went on for years. The major difference between them was that Fred Allen wrote most, if not all, of his own material while Benny wrote virtually none of his. To his credit, Benny never tried to claim otherwise, and it led to one of Benny's most generous tributes to Allen during one of their arguments: "You wouldn't dare talk to me that way if my writers were here."

At various times Allen said Benny "couldn't ad-lib a belch at a Hungarian picnic," and Benny retorted that until Allen was born, "nobody knew what a cramp looked like." Allen also said of Benny's violin playing that the strings would have been better off left in the cat.

The stable of characters on the shows became part of the landscape of our lives. We knew that Benny's wife, Mary Livingston, would join with their black chauffeur, Rochester, to keep Benny's ego deflated. We knew that sometime on the show Sheldon Leonard, who later became a pioneering television producer, would appear with his trademark, "Psst! Hey, bub . . . c'mere," and that bandleader Phil Harris would make his presence known with his jaunty "Hi-ya, Jackson," and would verbally flail Benny for being so cheap.

Allen had an equally mixed and talented cast of characters. Who could ever forget Senator Claghorn, played by Kenny Delmar ("That's a joke, son"), who became the wonderful cartoon rooster, Foghorn Leghorn. Then there was Titus Moody, played by Parker Fennelly as a wimpy character who once said he was so anemic that when he cut his finger, it did not bleed; it just puckered and hissed. Mrs. Nussbaum, played by Minerva Pious, was a broadly stereotypical Jewish woman who constantly complained about her husband, Pierre.

Allen told us that his little Maine town was so dull that the tide went out and did not come back. A few years later, when television made its appearance, he detested it: "The reason why television is called a medium is because nothing on it is ever well done."

We all looked forward to Sunday programming. Listings in Saturday's newspapers told us that on Sunday we could hear the New York Philharmonic under the leadership of Artur Rodzinski as it played Shostakovich's First Symphony. Soloist for the program was the great pianist Artur Rubenstein, who would perform Brahms's Concerto in B-flat Major.

Also in the classical vein were the NBC String Symphony, led by Frank Black; a concert by the André Kostelanetz Orchestra, with Albert Spalding as violinist and the singer Eleanor Steber as guest; and the Metropolitan Opera "Auditions on the Air." Later in the evening we could hear "The Perfectionist's Hour" featuring Dohnanyi's Quartet No. 2 in D-flat Major, and on the "Symphonic Hour," Brahms's Variations on a Theme by Haydn and Sibelius's Symphony No. 4 in A Minor.

In the newspaper column "The Hit Song of the Week," Benny Goodman chose "Little Fool," by a new composer and singer from the Dakotas named Peggy Lee.

A poignant note in the *Chicago Tribune* reminded us that a new short-wave program called "Hello, Children" had been created especially for the thousands of British children evacuated to the United States and Canada to protect them from the constant bombings by Germany.

What most Americans did not know or had ignored was that Japan had been steadily building up its industrial strength. The Japanese bought millions of tons of scrap metal from the United States; hired experts on aviation, naval architecture, and armament; and sent their brightest students to America to study at our universities. In the meantime, the island nation remained remote and for the most part closed to all foreigners except those the Japanese imported to teach them contemporary technology and Western techniques.

In the Saturday, December 6, *Wall Street Journal,* the newspaper stated that the biggest threat to the defense program was the shortage of steel and scrap iron which was threatening to curtail steel production. The industry said timely help from the government was essential. To demonstrate how limited the supplies were, the newspaper proposed that the government issue a national appeal to "householders, farmers, everyone, to join in a government-led and -directed campaign to salvage scrap from every backyard and corner lot." This approach to solving the problem created by selling the metal to Japan throughout the 1930s would be used extensively throughout the war.

In the same issue the *Journal* noted that the country "has virtually no immediately available reservoir of workers left in most of the essential defense occupations," according to Lieutenant Colonel Joseph F. Bailey, chief of the labor division in the under secretary of war's office. Training schools for aircraft assemblers, mechanics, and inspectors were running ads for students in newspapers all over the country.

In his muckraking column that ran in newspapers around the country on December 7, 1941, Drew Pearson shed some light on the steel shortage with two items. One had to do with what he called a "giant horde of semimanufactured war materials" bound for Poland, Czechoslovakia, Holland, and Belgium, nations by then defeated and occupied by Germany. "Tons upon tons of steel bars, steel rods, steel sheets, ship plates, tin plate and copper wire" were sitting in warehouses and in boxcars because of government secrecy and bureaucratic foul-ups.

Pearson also noted that for years the heaviest foreign buyer of scrap iron had been Japan, and that the State Department had continued to permit the sales in spite of much public protesting. In later years it was discovered that between 1935 and 1940 the United States sold Japan some 200 million tons of scrap iron. Japan had been paying for this iron and steel with silk; trains consisting of boxcars filled with raw silk would leave West Coast ports, amid much fanfare, bound for mills in the Midwest and East that made silk stockings, suits, dresses, and scarves.

However, now that Japan had invaded China, trying to conquer that vast nation, more and more Americans were sympathizing with China. America had chosen China's side for a variety of reasons: We had been doing business with China for decades, China had permitted American missionaries to proselytize there, and Japan was clearly the aggressor. Another factor was the magnetism of the Chinese dictator Chiang Kai-shek and his beautiful wife, who were frequent visitors to America. In 1938 America extended $25 million in credit to China and placed an embargo on selling more aircraft to Japan. When Japan occupied Indochina in 1940, America finally stopped shipping gasoline, steel, iron, and rubber to Japan, which had no raw materials of its own.

Part of the change in America's policy must be credited to people who had feared Japan for years before the Pearl Harbor attack and who had preached this danger. It was a difficult mission because what they said sounded more like paranoia or racism than the report of a genuine threat. One prophet of the coming disaster was Henry S. Evans, a newspaperman and public relations counselor who, with two Chinese-American doctors, founded the American Bureau for Medical Aid to China. Evans was convinced that Japan would attack the United States, and had been working with various organizations and traveling through the Midwest trying to get America to stop sending iron and steel to Japan.

Although the organizations for which Evans worked were lumped with the isolationist movement, they were not really part of it. Evans said his main mission was to make America stop selling materials to Japan that could be used against China, and ultimately the United States, and that isolationism was never the issue.

Evans saw the isolationist movement firsthand because Kansas City, Missouri, where he was based, was the capital of the isolationist movement. As often as not, the isolationists attracted the angry and the lost—and many crackpots. One of their chief arguments was that we should let sleeping dogs lie; that if we did not bother Germany and Japan, they would not bother us. It was unthinkable to them that we would actually be attacked.

Evans frequently felt like a prophet without portfolio because people would not listen. He watched with increasing fear as the Nazis courted key American leaders and journalists. "The Nazis were feeding them the party line, and as too often happens, the correspondents were bowled over by the fine hospitality and friendships. That is why it is best to transfer foreign correspondents from the area in which they have the most expertise. H. V. Kaltenborn [the radio commentator] was in Czechoslovakia when Germany attacked it, and he said then that there would be no war in Europe. He believed the Nazi line.

"I don't think Charles Lindbergh showed a lot of resistance to the Nazis, either. They decorated him, you know."

One of Evans's biggest victories came in 1932, when he was able to have "The Tanaka Memorial" read on national radio by Syngman Rhee, recently elected president of Korea's provisional government. "The Tanaka Memorial" is one of the most famous documents related to World War II, and since no Westerner ever saw the original, nobody is absolutely certain of its contents or the exact statements in the debate that led to its being written. From what has been learned after the fact, the document began as a report from Prime Minister Tanaka Gi-ichi to Emperor Hirohito following a major debate of Japan's elders during a meeting held from June 27 to July 7, 1927. The elders had gathered to discuss the course Japan should take on the Asian continent. The primary question they were trying to resolve was whether Japan should cut Manchuria from the rest of China and claim it as Japanese territory. If Japan decided to take over the province, should it be done by military action or by economic exploitation? Some of the elders believed war was inevitable and the only way to accomplish its aim to acquire Manchuria. Prime Minister Tanaka argued in favor of continued economic infiltration and exploitation because he believed that was Emperor Hirohito's wish.

Records of the meeting revealed that Tanaka was challenged by General Muto Nobuyoshi, commander of the garrison in Manchuria, who seemed to think either course meant war. "Japan must be prepared to face a world war if such a drastic program is to be carried out," he warned. "To begin with, America will not tolerate it. . . . Are you prepared to cope with America and the eventuality of a world war?" Tanaka said he was. When a vote was taken at the end of the meeting, Tanaka's proposal won overwhelmingly, and the report he presented to Emperor Hirohito became known as "The Tanaka Memorial."

The exact contents of the statement were known only to the few Japanese leaders who read it. Chinese intelligence agents got bits and pieces of it and put together their version, which apparently was quite different from the real document. In fact, if Japanese accounts of its contents are accurate, the Chinese version was the total opposite of Tanaka's report. According to David Bergamini, author of *Japan's Imperial Conspiracy,* the

Chinese version "became one of the most famous documents in Japanese history—a pastiche of truths adding up to a gigantic forgery."

The Chinese version said the Japanese plan was to conquer Manchuria and Mongolia, occupy China, defeat the United States, and conquer the world. However, the Japanese say Tanaka actually warned Hirohito that if Japan tried to conquer mainland Asia, it would force a war between Japan and the United States, which he did not believe Japan could hope to win. According to Bergamini, the Chinese version permanently confused Western intelligence analysts.

Evans said a copy of the memorial (which would have to be the Chinese version, since nobody outside the Japanese government ever saw the entire authentic document) fell into American hands in an interesting manner. The Chinese gave a copy of their version to the Russians. Next, the American ambassador in Tokyo was in the Russian ambassador's office. The Russian had a copy face up on his desk, made certain his American counterpart knew what it was, then left the room long enough for the American to copy it.

It was this report that Syngman Rhee, whom Evans had met in Honolulu, read to a national radio audience on the Mutual Network in 1932. "When the Mutual people saw a copy of the speech Syngman Rhee was going to read, they said it wasn't very interesting and wanted me to help. So I was able to insert 'The Tanaka Memorial' into the speech. The official Japanese line was that the memorial was a forgery. About a year before Pearl Harbor I was called on to debate a member of the Japanese embassy on 'Radio Forum,' a popular program of the period, and we held the debate in Joplin, Missouri. He gave the official line, too: that Japan did not want war, but that it was building what he called a 'prosperity sphere.' "

Evans said he also showed a film about the Japanese atrocities in Nanking when Japan invaded it in 1937. These atrocities are among the worst committed by any army at any time in history, and much of it was preserved on film, both still and motion picture, by Japanese soldiers and American, British, and German residents in the area. One of the most damning collections of film was taken by the Reverend John Magee, who became chaplain at Yale after World War II.

Equally damning were the photographs taken by Japanese soldiers who participated in the atrocities. They sent their film to processing studios in Shanghai and other Chinese cities as casually as if they were on vacation. The Chinese photo lab technicians made extra copies and smuggled them out to the West.

Nanking fell on the night of December 12, 1937, after a long siege, and something like 290,000 of the 300,000 Nanking residents were captured and imprisoned. During the battle the Caucasian residents had been able to form a safety zone for themselves, which the Japanese honored; and it is their accounts and their photographs, supplemented by photographs taken by Japanese soldiers, that give a uniformly horrifying picture of how Japan conducted itself as victor.

The wishes of Tokyo were clear. Prince Asaka, Emperor Hirohito's uncle, gave explicit orders: Take no captives. The 80,000 Japanese troops began the atrocities the next day. Thousands and thousands of prisoners were herded into city squares, tied hand and foot, and taken to pens on the bank of the Yangtze River. At nightfall they were brought out and used for bayonet practice, for demonstrations in decapitation, and to test samurai swords (it was found that none could split a man from head to groin in one stroke).

As the six-week rape and massacre continued, the Japanese found more and more novel ways to kill people, such as burying them neck deep and leaving them to die. Infants were tossed into the air to land on bayonets. Other children were raped; young girls were used as prostitutes or simply raped and killed.

The Japanese soldiers did not bother the Westerners inside the safety zone, but they did violate the zone by going in after women at night. Much of this was recorded on the film taken by Reverend Magee, and more was on the negatives Japanese soldiers sent to Chinese processing shops. This was the film Evans was able to show in Kansas City, Missouri. Afterward, the National Guard commander in Kansas City told Evans that it was nothing but propaganda against the Japanese, and had he known what it was, he would have prevented it from being shown.

The terrible irony was that the isolationist movement used the film in its propaganda as proof that the Orient was such a terrible place that America should leave it alone.

The millions of tons of scrap iron and steel being sent to Japan concerned Evans the most, and it was this problem to which he devoted his considerable energies as a volunteer. Evans had the statistics on our scrap iron and steel shipments to Japan, and he did not like what he saw. He had no doubt that Japan would attack America, and "The Tanaka Memorial" led him to believe that it would be in Hawaii, because the document made it clear that if Japan had to fight to conquer China, then Japan would have to knock America out of the Pacific. Like many others, Evans also believed it would be an invasion rather than an air raid.

"I had served three years in the Army in Hawaii, and we had maneuvers and exercises on repelling an invasion. We believed they would land at Haleiwa on the opposite side of the island from Pearl Harbor.

"Meanwhile, Japanese tourists were photographing Pearl Harbor from a Dole pineapple roadside stand that overlooked Pearl Harbor . . . and we soldiers weren't permitted to take photos of any military base."

As he lectured around the Midwest against selling scrap iron and steel to Japan, Evans met with great corporate resistance. Companies like Sheffield Steel not only were selling material to Japan, they also were selling entire rolling mills so the Japanese could make their own steel.

"In New York they were tearing down the elevated structures, which were made of a very good grade of steel, and they were being shipped to Japan. It was a very curious situation: We weren't only shipping scrap iron and steel and oil, but we were sending material to build up the infrastructure for the maintenance of their navy.

"I was on the Stimson committee called the American Committee for Nonparticipation in Japanese Aggression. In the Midwest I simplified it to the Stop Arming Japan Committee, and had a great deal of success. We were able to sign up 25,000 members in spite of the opposition many Americans had to the isolationists, with whom we were often lumped. Our goal was to go to Washington and show Secretary of State Cordell Hull that he should abrogate the 1911 treaty between the U.S. and Japan that gave them most-favored trade status, and that if Hull did so, he would have the backing of a lot of people.

"My wife and I were in our apartment in Louisville, Kentucky, on December 7, having brunch, when we heard about the Pearl Harbor attack on the radio. Although I had been anticipating it for several years, I was still shell-shocked, as everybody else was."

Ed Sheehan, who arrived in Honolulu in the summer of 1940 to work in the shipyard and has lived there since, captured the sun-drenched atmosphere of Honolulu, Waikiki, and Pearl Harbor superbly in his book *Days of '41.* He grew up in a poor Boston family and, before getting the shipyard job, the greatest sum he had ever earned was $18 a week, most of which went into the family pot.

Sheehan remembers the island of Oahu as a culturally rich mixture of old Hawaii, China, Japan, America, and Portugal. The island smelled of fragrant flowers, spices, the sea, and its rich, red soil. Waikiki did not have a single traffic light, and much of it was still given over to palm groves. The largest hotel on Waikiki was the pink Royal Hawaiian. The road from Honolulu to Pearl Harbor ran through sugarcane fields and across the Keehi Lagoon marshes. Almost nobody in Honolulu hurried, and old men gathered every morning beneath trees in the parks and along Waikiki to play cribbage all day.

"Almost every cottage in Waikiki sat amid lush greenery, under coconut, monkeypod, mango or banyan trees," Sheehan wrote. "Panax hedges or flowering bushes served as token fences. Flowers grew as if uncontrollable; plumeria of rich and heavy scent, velvety hibiscus in warm colors, and bougainvillea flaming like sunsets in orange, red, and purple. Even at the height of its activity Waikiki was a place dozing in tropical brilliance, a broad strand of comfortable homes inhabited by people who moved unhurriedly and smiled easily. Overwhelmingly, one's neighbors were generous, kind and trusting. Waikikians rarely locked their doors. . . . You simply left the house, and came back hours, even days later, to find everything just as you had left it."

Tourism was already very important to the Territory of Hawaii, with Matson ships making the five-day voyage from Treasure Island outside San Francisco on a regular basis. Pan American, headed by Juan Trippe, had its fleet of massive flying boats called clippers going all over the world. On Saturday, December 6, the *Capetown Clipper* took off from Miami with thirty passengers to inaugurate service between the United States and Africa. The big plane would fly southeast to Puerto Rico, then on to Trinidad, then Belém, Brazil, the farthest-east city on the South American continent. From there it would go nonstop across the Atlantic to Leopoldville, Belgian Congo. The clipper was still en route when news came over the company radio system that Pearl Harbor, half a world away, was being attacked.

The inauguration of African service accomplished one thing for Pan American and something else for the Allies. Trippe had wanted to pioneer commercial airline service to Africa, and Churchill and Roosevelt wanted a route to ferry lend-lease planes to Europe without the risk of flying through the North Atlantic war zone. The government and Pan American struck a deal: In exchange for establishing a route and ground stations, Trippe would be given the African concession. He had also made himself more indispensable to the military by having his crews teach celestial navigation to Air Force and Navy flight crews.

In Hawaii, Pan American's eighteen-hour flight from the mainland was considered almost miraculously speedy, although Hawaiian Airlines had recently taken delivery of three DC-3 twenty-four-passenger planes that flew from Oakland to Honolulu in only thirteen hours and fifty-three minutes, a new speed record. Pan American was not very worried because the faster DC-3 could never compete with the clippers for comfort, which included the ability to turn each passenger compartment into a bedroom, much like railroad Pullman cars.

The Pan American clippers were remarkable aircraft. Trippe told friends he had a dream as a child that he was riding on what he thought was a ship, then discovered it was a luxurious airplane. The dream had stayed with him through college and until he established his airline. Then he designed the kind of plane he needed to make his dream literally come true. The first clipper was built by Sikorsky; the others, by Martin and Boeing. They were an immediate sensation.

The one-way fare from San Francisco to Honolulu was $278, or $500.40 round trip. The four-engine planes left Treasure Island every Wednesday at 4 P.M. and arrived in Honolulu at about 8 A.M. the following morning. They had five standard passenger compartments plus a luxurious one in the rear of the plane called the honeymoon suite.

Trippe was constantly scouting out new routes in his effort to make Pan American the dominant air carrier in the world. The transpacific route was relatively new, and it had been inaugurated as a result of Trippe's single-mindedness. Not content to fly to Honolulu, he wanted to fly both the breadth and the length of the Pacific.

Trippe's clippers were large. Although they carried an enormous load of fuel, the four engines consumed so much that more had to be taken on somewhere between Hawaii and the Asian mainland. The small atoll of Wake Island had always been there, but hardly anyone except a handful of government cartographers and military planners knew of its existence. The only Americans who seemed to care were those planning the eventual laying of a transpacific telephone cable. Otherwise, it was deemed useless: no trees, no water; just sand and coral. To make the place even more dismal, the men stationed there complained that most of the fish in the lagoon were not safe to eat.

Wake was perfect for Trippe because it was 2,300 miles west of Honolulu and 1,290 miles east of Guam on a direct line between Honolulu and Hong Kong. It was also almost halfway between Midway and Guam.

Wake had been named for the British captain who discovered it in 1796 but did not bother to claim it. The United States did so in 1899 with the transpacific cable in mind, then put it on some charts and ignored it. When Trippe's staff found it on charts, Trippe asked the government if he could build a base there. Nobody in Washington had the faintest idea what to tell him because no agency had ever administered it. They could not even tell him where to apply for the permit.

Trippe eventually got the permit and sent out a ship loaded with building materials, food, fuel, and a construction crew to blast away the coral and build a base, complete with a hotel for the passengers and crew. As the tensions rose between the United States and Japan, a military base and landing strip for Navy planes and a detachment of Marines was built on another island in the atoll.

Americans assumed two things: that the national economy would keep getting better and that the war situation would get worse. We did not necessarily connect the two, in part because most Americans preferred not to believe the events in Europe and Asia would directly involve America. We knew England was taking a pounding—she had already suffered 14,000 civilian deaths and 20,000 injured in the German air attacks—and we knew we were helping as much as we could.

In the White House, President Roosevelt knew all of these things, and he was positive America would be at war in a very short time. He hoped he could hold the Axis at bay until America's arsenal was built. Most of the airplanes were going from the end of the production lines to England and across the Pacific to our allies. Our warship construction program was moving, but not as fast as events. Roosevelt was trying, in his words, to "baby along" Japan and to support England until he had a stronger hand to play. If he could stay out of war until April 1942. . . .

If anyone could pull America into a European war on the basis of friendship, it would be Great Britain. Long before Pearl Harbor we had been helping the British with both men and material. Many young Americans, particularly pilots, crossed into Canada to join military units bound for Great Britain. One recruiting officer in Toronto said that before America entered the war, he signed up between 300 and 400 men, most of whom were university students and nearly all of whom wanted into the Air Force. Most, he noted, were drunk or hung over when they arrived. Consequently, when America entered the war, many Americans were already serving in Canadian units.

This close relationship with Britain and President Roosevelt's ability to circumvent laws he did not like created a strange footnote to the prewar period. Congress had enacted several laws to prevent Roosevelt from getting too involved in the European war. The Neutrality Act of 1935 forbade the shipment in "American bottoms" (American-made ships) of war material to any belligerent in a declared war. Also, the material could be had on a cash-and-carry basis only. Nor could credit be extended to any nation in default of its debts from World War I.

Roosevelt found imaginative ways of getting around these laws. One of the most famous was getting airplanes to Britain and France. Although it occurred at other places along the Canadian border, the best-documented case was on the international boundary between Houlton, Maine, and Woodstock, New Brunswick. The stipulation was simple to circumvent: The airplanes could not be flown across the international boundary, but the law did not say they could not be pushed, pulled, or hauled across. The Works Progress Administration lengthened the runway at Houlton's airport, then the planes began arriving. Some were flown up and others were brought by train and truck. Once there, they were towed down the two-lane highway from Houlton to the airport at Woodstock, a distance of about twelve miles. At first the old biplane dive bombers were hauled on trucks, but there were too many planes and not enough trucks, so they were towed down the road by cars, trucks, farm tractors, and even horses and mules. From the Woodstock airstrip, they were flown across the Bay of Fundy to Nova Scotia and the field at Halifax, and loaded onto ships headed for Europe.

The first big shipment was to fill an order placed by the French government for as many of the Curtiss planes as the factory could produce, with the total expected to reach 1,600. The planes were as good as promised, and in September 1939, the French won their only air victory with Curtiss fighters.

The French soon ran out of American dollars, and gold was the only other currency the American government could accept. The first gold shipment, some 100 tons, arrived in Halifax aboard the battleship *Lorraine.* This was followed by shipments of 250 tons and 400 tons; another 300 tons was aboard a cruiser that was diverted to Martinique after the French government fell to the Germans.

Just before Germany took France and the Low Countries, America rushed more Curtiss Helldiver bombers into production in the plant at Buffalo, declared them "surplus" so they could be sold to the French, then camouflaged them and flew them to Houlton to be dragged into Canada and flown off to war.

The last shipment of these Helldivers was loaded onto the aircraft carrier *Béarn,* France's only carrier completed before war broke out. The *Béarn* left Halifax for home with 106 biplanes just as France fell to the Germans. The captain did not know what to do, so he took the ship to the French island of Martinique to wait for instructions—or perhaps divine inspiration. To his chagrin, his ship and its cargo became the focal point of an international incident as attempts were made by various governments, particularly those of England, France, and America, to claim the planes and to rule the island. Neither America nor England really wanted the island; they just did not want the Germans or the puppet government they had installed in France to take possession of Martinique.

The English wanted the 106 planes desperately, and on July 6, 1940, laid claim to them and blockaded the Martinique harbor. The United States protested, and in the summer of 1940 sent a cruiser and six destroyers and placed a detachment of Marines on standby alert. As one observer later wrote, "Thus, by mid-July there emerged the ludicrous spectacle of an American force keeping tabs on a British force which was blockading a possession of a former ally, all at a time when both navies had many more important things to do."

America sent a wise negotiator, Rear Admiral John W. Greenslade, to Martinique, to strike a gentlemen's agreement with the French on the island: The island would remain under French control but everything of military value, including ships, airplanes, and gold to pay for the planes, would remain on the island; an American adviser would be on site throughout the war. In return, America would provide Martinique with food and medical supplies.

After the Allied forces took North Africa, America severed diplomatic relations with the French Vichy puppet regime and cut off supplies to Martinique. The results were disastrous for the islanders, who sometimes supplemented bread with sawdust, and had to resort to burning rum to fuel their cars. The Vichy crackdown was so severe that anyone caught listening to an Allied radio broadcast was imprisoned. There followed an evacuation; people paid fishermen up to $200 a head for the thirty-eight-mile passage to St. Lucia.

As Saturday ended across America, we went to bed confident and secure, and not particularly concerned when we heard on the radio that President Roosevelt had cut short his vacation in Warm Springs, Georgia, to return to Washington, D.C. In Memphis and New Orleans, in Chicago and San Francisco, in the hotels along Miami Beach and on Coronado Island, the hotel bands played one last slow number—"At Last," "There's a Tree in the Meadow," "I'll Be Seeing You," "Moonlight Serenade," or "Stardust"—to clear the dance floors and send people home in a romantic mood.

Ed Sheehan, the Boston boy working in the shipyards, was spending that Saturday night working in drydock 1, where the destroyers *Downes* and *Cassin* were being rebuilt beneath the looming presence of the battleship *Pennsylvania.*

"Cranes dropped the new plates down to us, and we fought them into place with crowbars and sledgehammer blows," he wrote in *Days of '41.* "Welders made blinding contact, and bright streams of molten metal cascaded down to bounce off the drydock floor. The intense blue-white light sent great shadows dancing upon the dock's walls. The air was almost still, and smoke gathered in the low pocket until it was oppressive. Frequently we had to wait for the haze to rise and be blown away.

"During a break I went inside the *Downes* to cadge some coffee. A chief bosun's mate had the duty, and we sat in the chief petty officers' quarters drinking a thick brew. He was addressing Christmas cards with troubled pauses, his brow furrowed and pen poised. He said he was writing the same goddam thing on all the goddam cards and asked me for some ideas. I remember teaching him how to spell Merry Christmas in Hawaiian, 'Mele Kalikimaka.' "

For Sheehan, it was just another Saturday night spent working instead of walking the streets, checking out the single girls on Waikiki, or seeing a movie.

Military readiness hardly existed in Hawaii then. Until he was relieved by Admiral Husband Kimmel in early 1941, the former fleet commander, Admiral James Richardson, had kept his ships at the ready. He did not like Pearl Harbor; he considered it a trap. He knew that if a surprise attack came, it would take at least three hours to clear the ships from the harbor. In other words, it was an impossibility. He had often complained that Pearl Harbor was too small for a hundred ships and that recreational facilities for his men were inadequate. He had argued with President Roosevelt against moving the fleet from San Diego to Hawaii the previous year, and when he was ordered to do so, he did his best to protect the fleet by keeping it in Laihana Roads, the stretch of ocean surrounded by Maui, Molokai, Lanai, and the smaller Kahoolawe. There would be no trapping the fleet here because it had no bottlenecks, no entrances to mine or to close with a sunken ship.

All of this made Richardson an increasingly unpopular figure in Hawaii and in Washington, D.C. Wives complained to their congressmen and anyone who would listen that they could not see their husbands. Their husbands returned from the occasional weekend liberty disgruntled from listening to their wives complain all weekend. Worst of all, reenlistments were dropping at a time when the Navy wanted to keep as many experienced men on the ships as possible. Naturally the admiral was blamed for everything. In addition, Honolulu merchants were complaining that the admiral was costing them a fortune.

Admiral Richardson was not at all concerned about these things. His only interest was his fleet's readiness and safety. Consequently, he was soon replaced by the more congenial Admiral Kimmel, whose first action was to move the fleet into Pearl Harbor. So anxious was he to improve morale that he began operating the fleet on schedules. The ships went out on Monday and returned on Friday. In the case of a longer exercise, the ships went out on a Friday and returned eight days later, on a Saturday. This soothed the wives and merchants. It also made the Navy totally predictable for Japanese spies.

On the Army side, General Walter C. Short, commanding general of Hawaii, was hardly better prepared. He had been trying to get his troops properly trained, and he had been keeping them on alerts as the Japanese threat increased. However, it is impossible to keep servicemen on alert for long periods of time without boredom, resentment, and disbelief setting in. The alerts had begun in the summer and drifted on through the fall, and General Short knew he had to do something to keep the troops' morale from plummeting.

He developed three types of alerts to replace the Army's one-alert system. His alerts began with the lowest priority, which was designed to prevent sabotage. The next one, slightly more serious, was designed as a defense against an air attack. And finally there was the all-out alert, to be used in the event of an invasion.

Oddly, although General Short and Admiral Kimmel had tried to coordinate all their efforts, they neglected to coordinate the alerts. The Army's three-stage alert system was now like that of the Navy, except that their numbering systems were the exact opposites of each other.

Thus, on that weekend the ships, planes, and shore batteries had been on and off alerts over the past several days and the edge of fear of attack had been blunted by the failure of an enemy to appear. Most military personnel believed that if the Japanese did attack, it would be somewhere else. The bases were on the lowest-level alert status, and the warplanes were lined up away from the buildings, out in the open in neat rows, to make it difficult for saboteurs to get to them. This was perfect for the dive bombers and fighters that would soon arrive.

1

The First Shot

The role played by two destroyers, the *Ward* and the *Henley,* illustrates how quickly men adapted to the new situation. Men who have served on ships can appreciate the words of Donald K. Ross, who won a Medal of Honor for ordering his men out and staying at his post in the engine room of the battleship *Nevada* when it seemed certain he would die. "We give our souls to the ship, and she becomes a living thing to us," he said.

On that day hard men shed tears when they saw how badly their beloved ships were damaged, and it was that love of their ships, as much as anger at the Japanese, that kept many of them going.

The war actually began before dawn on December 7 when the aging destroyer *Ward* was steaming back and forth, covering a two-mile-square patch of restricted water across the entrance of the channel into Pearl Harbor. The *Ward* was one of about two hundred destroyers built in 1918, and for years she held the record for speed of construction at Mare Island in San Francisco Bay: She was launched seventeen days after the keel was laid.

The ship had been in Pearl Harbor since February, and during those months the crew had spent a lot of time at sea on patrol and in training. At least eighty members of the crew were from a reserve unit from St. Paul-Minneapolis; they had received thorough training during the past ten months and were ready for a fight.

The *Ward* was commanded by Lieutenant William W. Outerbridge, who was on his first patrol on his first command; he had taken over the ship from her previous skipper, Lieutenant Commander Hunter Wood, on Friday, December 5. His last assignment had been as executive officer on the destroyer *Cummings,* and he had spent some time aboard battleships before that. Outerbridge later said he had fallen in love with his ship the day he went aboard her, and he retained that special affection throughout his life. All of the *Cummings*'s officers except one were U.S. Naval Academy graduates. Now Outerbridge was the only Academy graduate on a ship filled with reserve officers.

The new skipper was different in other ways. He was the son of an English merchant captain and an American mother. Outerbridge, thirty-five years old in 1941, was born and reared in Hong Kong. When his father died, his mother took him back to her native Ohio. He won an appointment to the Naval Academy, from which he graduated in the class of 1927. He was short, about five-foot-five, and stocky; Joseph A. Groden, who later served with him, said Outerbridge reminded him of a Kewpie doll. In 1941 he was one of many junior officers who had been suffering through the doldrums of the 1930s, waiting for something to happen so he could get a ship and move up the chain of command.

Outerbridge was also known as an officer who was not afraid to make a decision. On the morning of December 7, he had to make several.

That long day began at 3:42 A.M. when Ensign R. C. McCloy, aboard the minesweeper *Condor* on routine patrol off the entrance to Pearl Harbor, spotted the periscope of a two-man submarine. His discovery was signaled to the *Ward,* cruising nearby. The officer of the deck, Lieutenant (j.g.) Oscar W. Goepner, called Outerbridge out of bed. The skipper went to the bridge, had a quick look around, and called the crew to General Quarters. The old destroyer raced over on the attack.

The two ships circled the area but found nothing, so Outerbridge canceled General Quarters and two-thirds of the crew went back to bed at 4:43 A.M. Outerbridge stretched out on a couch in the chart room off the bridge. Neither ship reported the event to headquarters, and neither did a shore station listening in on the search. Since the sighting was not definite, nobody thought it was worth reporting. It actually was the first of many errors in judgment that day, although the other preattack events give one reason to doubt it would have made any difference in the outcome.

At about 6:30 A.M. the crew of a Catalina flying boat (PBY) on patrol reported that a submarine was trailing a supply ship, the *Antares,* which was headed into the mouth of Pearl Harbor. The *Antares* was returning from a supply run to Palmyra Island with a lighter in tow. The two PBY aviators, Ensign William Tanner and his copilot, Ensign Clark Greevey, knew no submarines were supposed to be operating in the area, no matter what their nationality. Assuming it was an American submarine in distress, they dropped two smoke pots to mark its position, then radioed their discovery to Pearl Harbor.

At about the same time, lookouts on both the *Ward* and the *Antares* spotted the sub. At first Goepner, who still had the *Ward* watch, thought it was just debris in the water, an orange crate perhaps, but Seaman H. E. Raenbig, at the helm, told him that whatever it was, it was moving. Convinced now, Goepner shouted to Outerbridge, and the skipper appeared on the bridge, wearing the brightly colored kimono he always used as a dressing gown. One of his men said he looked like a samurai. Outerbridge asked the teenage sonar technician, Robert H. Gorman, to confirm that it really was a sub. Gorman said it was.

"What are we going to do, Captain?" asked the gunner, a chief petty officer.

"We're going to shoot," Outerbridge replied. Outerbridge and his executive officer, Lieutenant Hartwell W. Doughty, briefly discussed the political ramifications of shooting at the submarine. Before he had taken command of the *Ward,* Outerbridge had made a careful study of the American battle plans, and they were specific in defense of the entrance to Pearl Harbor. If the vessel did not belong there, it was to be considered hostile and should be attacked.

Outerbridge announced to the men on the bridge that he didn't give a damn if it was an American, German, or Japanese sub; he was going to sink it because it was not supposed to be in the restricted zone.

He hit the General Quarters alarm and the ship went back to battle stations. He rang up "all engines ahead full," then told the helmsman to come left. The ship heeled over and went to war at about half speed because two of the four boilers were cold. The sailors on deck watched their claim to history unfolding. It is doubtful the submarine saw the *Ward* approaching, because it kept on its steady pace behind the *Antares* with no change in speed or course. The *Ward* sailors could see the barnacles on the sub's hull and moss on the conning tower. When the *Ward* was about 100 yards away, Outerbridge gave the order to commence firing. It was about 6:45 A.M. They were too close to use the gunsights, so the gunners had to aim by sighting down the barrels.

Thus America's first shot of World War II was fired by a destroyer commanded by a man wearing a kimono.

The first shot missed, but the *Ward* gunners were on target the next time; they saw the second shot hit the conning tower, causing the sub to heel over, but it kept going on the same course. Outerbridge continued toward the submarine and shouted down the voice tube to the engine room to be prepared to ram. But he changed his mind at the last minute and raced past the submarine, missing it by about thirty feet, still so close that the *Ward*'s wake spun the little craft. Outerbridge gave four blasts on the ship's whistle to order four depth charges. The chief torpedoman, W. C. Maskzawilz, set them to detonate at 100 feet and dropped them as the destroyer passed the submarine. The setting was very shallow and could have blown off the *Ward*'s own fantail if she had not been moving away fast enough.

When the depth charges exploded, they lifted the destroyer's stern into the air and popped the screws that held the sheet-metal floor plates in the fireroom and engine room, terrifying the crews down there who could not see any of the action and had no idea what was going to happen when.

Nobody saw the submarine again. Maskzawilz was sure the first charge went off right under it. Outerbridge, still clad in his kimono, reported his attack in code to headquarters. Two minutes later, when he failed to get an enthusiastic response, or even a slightly interested response, he sent a more specific follow-up message: "Attacked, fired on, depth-bombed, and sunk, submarine operating in defensive area." He hoped the stronger words "fired on" and "sunk" would command some respect. Nothing of the sort happened. The radioman received meaningless messages: repeat, confirm, clarify, and so on. Outerbridge was livid.

On shore, the message was received, then decoded, then delivered to the watch officer about twenty minutes later. Not until about 7:30 was Admiral Kimmel finally told.

In the meantime the *Ward* continued its busy morning. At 6:48 A.M., only three minutes after attacking the submarine, the destroyer found a white sampan in the restricted area and went over to seize and hold it while waiting for the Coast Guard to tow it to their station. When the destroyer bore down on the little vessel, smoke pouring from its funnels, battle flag flying and oil and debris from its previous victim floating in the ocean behind it, the sampan skipper was justifiably terrified and began frantically waving a white flag. Some seamen believed it was unusual for a civilian sailor to wave the flag of surrender, and some still believe the sampan was out there shielding the submarine from the view of the destroyer. But no evidence has ever been found to support that contention. Instead, the general assumption is that with all the warfare going on around him, the skipper was completely justified in using the white flag, or any other symbol of surrender, to keep from being attacked.

The Coast Guard cutter arrived and had hardly begun the tow before everyone was attacked by the incoming Japanese planes. "The last we saw of the cutter, it was zigging and zagging like mad and being bombed by the Japanese," said Gorman.

As soon as Outerbridge saw that the war had started, he ordered steam up on all four boilers, and put his crew to work on the ship's limited number of guns. Then three very dangerous things happened. In one evasive maneuver, the chief quartermaster, watching incoming aircraft and trying to evade their bombs or torpedoes, was not watching the rudder indicator and turned it all the way to port, causing it to lock so that the destroyer ran in circles for a brief time. At the same time, the engine room men, excited and frightened, lost the oil pressure on the two boilers that were already on line. For perhaps fifteen minutes the *Ward* was helpless and had black smoke belching from her four stacks while the engine room staff got her fired up again.

Then, to compound the confusion, one of the three-inch guns that was just below the bridge hung fire. It was manned by mess attendants and cooks, who had less training than most deck crews. The muzzle was pointed straight up, and when the charge exploded, it sent a sheet of fire up past the bridge. It caused no damage, but when one sailor saw the flame shoot up, he shouted, "My God! We're hit!"

A lookout in Pearl Harbor saw the billowing smoke, the helpless circling, and the apparent explosion on board and also reported that the ship had been hit.

Outerbridge was furious at this turn of events. He had reported, repeatedly, that the war had begun, and all he got in return was meaningless messages. All messages were being transmitted in code rather than plain English, and it took precious minutes to decode and relay them to the proper authorities, who did very little. When he did get a response, it was to order another destroyer into the area and a standby destroyer to build up a head of steam, or for him to repeat the previous message or to confirm previous message or to stand by. By the time someone listened to him, it was too late.

So the men on the *Ward* watched most of the battle from the sea, occasionally being strafed or bombed by a Japanese plane; but for the most part they were spectators making figure eights back and forth across the channel entrance in search of more submarines and watching for the naval fleet everyone assumed would follow behind the air attack.

At about noon Outerbridge took the *Ward* into Pearl Harbor to refuel and to take on provisions and ammunition; the supply of depth charges was particularly low. The crew was silent, and most were crying as they slipped slowly past the destruction: airplanes on Ford Island burned to their skeletons, fire fighters still pumping water into the burning vessels, ships upside down, ships and boats milling around.

Seeing the destruction made Outerbridge even angrier about the failure of his messages to get through, and he stormed into headquarters to demand that somebody explain why this had happened. He was turned back at the door; nobody wanted to talk to a lowly lieutenant who commanded a beat-up old tin can. However, he later was given one of the forty-nine Naval Crosses awarded for heroism that day.

The *Ward* went back on patrol that evening, the crew feeling very lonely and small. When the destroyer passed the submarine net tenders at the mouth of the harbor, they cheered. Other ships were out with the *Ward,* but they were a platoon against what everyone suspected was an entire navy. Outerbridge was still angry about everything that had happened that day, and he told his crew that if they did find the Japanese fleet, they were not going to bother with the picket ships protecting the larger carriers; they were going into the middle to get the ships that really counted.

"We were really frightened," said Robert H. Gorman, the young sonarman. "We were so sure we were going to catch it that the storekeeper handed out cigarettes, free. Of course, when we lived, he had to make up the shortage out of his own pocket, but that night he didn't care."

The destroyer made several sonar contacts with submarines and dropped 172 depth charges over the next week of patrol, but made no confirmed kills.

History served up some irony regarding Outerbridge and his first command. As the war wore on, he was transferred to the destroyer *O'Brien* and was in a battle in Leyte Gulf in December 1944, when the *Ward* was mortally wounded and had to be sunk. By a freakish coincidence, Outerbridge had the sad duty of sinking his beloved *Ward* on December 7, 1944—exactly three years from the day he had fired the first shots of the war from the ship.

2

The Americans Fight Back

Nobody knows the exact minute the first bomb fell on Pearl Harbor, but the generally accepted time is 7:55 A.M. However, the first Japanese bullets hit Hawaii a few minutes earlier when fighters strafed Kaneohe Naval Air Station, almost due north of Honolulu, returned and strafed the amphibious base again, then bombed about half an hour later. Three of the station's thirty-six planes were on patrol; and twenty-seven of the remaining thirty-three were destroyed on the ground and the other six were damaged. Other planes hit Wheeler Field in the middle of the island, destroying forty-two planes and damaging the rest. These attackers then joined the others at Pearl Harbor and Hickam Field.

Very little damage was done to Bellows Field near Waimanalo. No bombs were dropped on it, but it was strafed by a group of planes that destroyed three of the craft on the ground. The only military target untouched was the new emergency field at Haleiwa because the Japanese apparently did not know it existed.

The major damage was done by the first wave of planes. Each of the seven battleships was hit then, and the *Arizona* and the *West Virginia* sank. The *Tennessee* was only slightly damaged. The *California*'s stern was resting on the bottom. The *Nevada* managed to get under way but was badly damaged, and was beached rather than block the channel. The *Oklahoma* capsized when four torpedoes hit her. The *Pennsylvania* was badly damaged.

Several hundred men were killed and wounded at Hickam Field when bombs and bullets hit the barracks. Bombs also hit the guardhouse, disabling the air raid siren. The ordnance building also was hit, holding up the distribution of firearms for a few precious minutes. The machine shop, hangars, theater, parade ground, and post exchange were all damaged.

Two harmless targets were hard hit, each apparently because of a misunderstanding. The bombers and torpedo planes concentrated much of their firepower on the *Pennsylvania,* which was in dry dock and looked vaguely like a carrier, and the baseball diamond at Schofield Barracks was riddled with machine-gun fire and bombs because the Japanese had an old map of the area that showed a gasoline storage area there.

The soldiers and sailors on land responded very quickly to the attack; it took only seven minutes for most of the antiaircraft batteries on ships to start firing. An antiaircraft battery on Sand Island was credited with two Japanese planes. Men on ship and shore fired anything they could find—rifles, pistols, machine guns—and some ignored regulations and broke into arsenals for firearms. One sailor threw hand tools at the planes as they flew past. Some stripped machine guns from damaged or destroyed planes. A few planes managed to get into the air, and by the day's end the Army pilots had made eighty-one takeoffs. Most were from Bellows Field, Haleiwa, and Wheeler.

Events of the day became a series of vignettes, all related to the crisis at hand but neither organized nor planned. Men and women reacted to the shock instinctively, and all survivors say essentially the same thing: People handled themselves very well, almost always with bravery.

Thomas A. Lombardi, an ensign aboard the *West Virginia,* was courting Martha Wing, a Boston girl living in Honolulu. On that Saturday night they had attended a dinner dance at the Officers' Club at Pearl Harbor, and by the time he had taken her home to Waikiki by bus and taxi and returned to Pearl Harbor, he had missed the last boat back to the ship. The next would be at 8 A.M.

"Along with several other young ensigns we got what little sleep we could at the landing, and as we were getting into the boat at 7:55, one of the ensigns, Bert English, saw a flight of planes over the air station dead ahead and said, 'The skipper [of the air station] must be mad at the fly boys; he has them out practicing early on Sunday morning.'

"Just as he said this, we saw a big explosion on the air station, and at the same time heard a roar overhead. We looked up to see a Japanese torpedo plane zooming down the channel leading to our ships half a mile away, followed by many others, one after the other. Although we were stupefied, we saw what was happening and shoved off to head back to the ship. By the time we reached it, she had been hit by seven torpedoes and three bombs, and had settled into the mud, decks awash. We were lucky we weren't strafed on the way across.

"Most of the damage caused by the Japanese occurred in the first fifteen minutes, so things were happening so fast that when we reached our ship, the *Arizona,* moored behind us, had blown up and most of the moored battleships had been sunk or damaged. All we could do when we got aboard was tend the wounded and fight the fires.

"I was in a tuxedo and light pumps, which gave little protection from the deck that was hot from the fires. Luckily, a pair of rubber boots just my size, 13, were lying on the forecastle. I put them on and solved the hot-foot problem. But what a battle uniform—white tuxedo shirt and black rubber boots!"

Like tornado stories in the Midwest, almost any story told about the attack can be accepted as truth. Who could invent a story like what happened to Admiral Kimmel as he stood at a window watching the attack that meant the end of his career?

A spent bullet crashed through the window and hit him in the chest, then tumbled to the floor. He picked it up and recognized it as a .50-caliber machine-gun bullet.

"It would have been more merciful had it killed me," he told an aide.

Ralph E. Pottker was a young lieutenant (j.g.) aboard the light cruiser *Phoenix.* His wife, Olga, remained in Illinois because he had insisted on it.

"We hadn't been married very long," she recalled, "and I wasn't happy about being separated at all. But I went to Peoria, where his mother lived, and got a job selling advertising on the *Peoria Journal.*"

At that time, Pottker was off the ship attending an antiaircraft gunnery school at Puuloa Point near Pearl Harbor, and he did not think much of the living conditions.

"It was rather unpleasant duty," he recalled later. "It meant living in tents in a sandy, isolated area, and the meals consisted mainly of Spam and cabbage. Not surprisingly, my first Sunday's leave was going to be spent looking for a good hotel with a fine restaurant, far away from the training area."

Pottker woke early that Sunday morning, walked over to Hickam Field, and caught a bus into Honolulu. At almost exactly 8 A.M., he walked into the lobby of the Alexander Young Hotel. He was relishing the thought of getting a room, buying a newspaper, and treating himself to a fine breakfast.

Then he heard about the attack, which hardly surprised him. He joined up with two other naval officers, dashed out of the hotel, and flagged down a cab. They ordered the driver to take them to Pearl Harbor and to turn on his radio. When the driver heard of the attack, he refused to take them to Pearl Harbor. The three young officers began ejection proceedings against him, telling him the cab was going there with or without him.

"Okay, Okay," he conceded. "I'm an American, too. I'll take you."

He did, and when they were strafed by Zeros on the way there, the driver hunched his shoulders and kept driving. He got them to the small-boat landing without being hit.

While they stood at the boat landing, waiting for a launch and watching the ships burn, Pottker looked around. Beside him stood a friend he had been trying to get in touch with for months. With bombs falling and bullets hitting all around them, they pumped hands and slapped shoulders.

The *Phoenix* got under way and circled the islands for three days before returning to refuel.

"We were wrenched with the desolate sight before us," Pottker said. "All of the sunken and burning ships were still in view, but there was an added horrible sight of the Navy tugboats towing barges literally piled high with the bodies of the men who were killed in the attack. We viewed the victims' bodies as they were carried to a nearby landing, hosed down to remove the gore and to be identified, and then put into hastily made wooden boxes.

"Awaiting them was a long line of trucks of all descriptions—beer trucks, grocery vans, any kind of conveyance which had been commandeered to take away the dead for burial at the U.S. National Military Cemetery."

Cab drivers were almost as busy dodging bombs and bullets as the servicemen who were piling into cabs all over Honolulu. To their credit, most of the cabbies performed like crewmen on landing craft; they kept going back for more.

Larry Katz, a radio operator at the seaplane base on Ford Island, was recovering from a night on the town when the attack came. He and two friends, Harold Donahue and George Soloff, had closed the Rendezvous Club on Waikiki Beach and had gone back to Honolulu for the night.

They could not find a hotel room, so they went to Battleship Max Cohen's locker club across the street from the downtown YMCA and the Black Cat Café.

"We slept on top of the lockers that night in our civvies," Katz said. "About 7 A.M. we got up and went to the café for breakfast, and after breakfast went for a walk in the park across the street.

"About that time we saw the planes and the antiaircraft bursts, and a window right above us blew out from the concussions of the bombs dropping and the guns going off. Then someone told us that they had heard all military men were to report back to their bases immediately.

"We jumped into a cab and had our driver speed back to the Navy yard so we could get a launch back to Ford Island. We kept seeing planes and smoke from Battleship Row, but until then we honestly did not know what was going on. But when we got to Hickam Field on the way to the yard, we saw B-17s trying to take off but never did see one get off the ground.

"I was sitting on the starboard side of the cab, Donahue in the middle and Soloff on the port side, my arm around Donahue's shoulder, when we heard a tack-tack-tack sound behind us. I turned and saw a plane coming down the road with tracers coming out of the wings, and realized we were being strafed. About the time the plane caught up with us, it swung to the right of the highway and made a run down the Hickam Field runway. The plane was a 'Val' and had the meatball on the side, a diagonal stripe running down the fuselage, and fixed landing gear with pants over the wheels.

"I was close enough to see the face of the Japanese pilot, and until my dying day I will never forget it.

"We got to the Navy yard after the cab driver veered off the road, and we ran the rest of the way. We couldn't get over to Ford Island because all hell was breaking loose. We had no direction of what to do, and we just looked around to help any way we could. We got to the USS *Pennsylvania,* which was between the *Cassin* and *Downes,* and tried to help out there.

"Then another attack came, and I dove in a hole and tried to cover myself with rocks or anything loose, because stuff was falling all around us. When I finally came up, I saw Donahue under a flatcar loaded with sixteen-inch shells which I think were to go aboard the *Pennsylvania.* We laugh about it now, but it was no laughing matter then.

"Just then the USS *Nevada* was trying to get out of the channel when it got hit. The skipper of that ship did the greatest thing I saw; he headed the *Nevada* right up on the beach. I heard a loud roar coming from our men, and it was the proudest moment of the day for me.

"I finally got back to Ford Island about four that afternoon and went right back to my radio station and stayed on duty all night, sleeping on the floor of the radio shack. The next morning I went to the sick bay to see a dud that was dropped right in the center of the hospital courtyard. It was the most eerie thing I had ever seen.

"So the three of us got through the attack without being hurt, and we stayed together through the whole war."

Marion M. Brown, a member of the 14th Naval District Band at Pearl Harbor, was living in the receiving barracks with a view across the Navy yard and parts of Pearl Harbor and Battleship Row.

He had just awakened and was sitting on his top bunk, feet dangling over, when he heard an explosion and saw a cloud of black smoke rising from about where the *Curtiss* (AV-4), on which he had just served, was tied up. At first he thought the aviation gasoline on her had exploded. But then he saw a low-wing fighter swoop by with an orange ball on its fuselage and a torpedo dangling under it. Then he saw the torpedo drop and watched as it hit a battleship.

Brown got dressed, and when a lull came, someone came in and said people were needed on the battleship *Pennsylvania,* so he ran down to where she sat in dry dock.

"I went below decks and started helping pass sixteen-inch shells up to the gun turrets, but no one had stopped to think that sixteen-inch guns couldn't be fired in dry dock.

"At the next lull I decided to get out of there. When I got topside and saw what happened right there in the dry dock, I almost died. I started back to the receiving station when the last wave of planes came over. I dove into a lumber pile, and there I stayed until it was over.

"Back at the receiving station, a gunner's mate and I were given a .30-caliber machine gun and told to guard a power transformer. That night a carrier plane tried to land, and every gun in the harbor fired at it.

"We fired, too, but nothing happened. When we put the gun together, we failed to assemble it correctly and it couldn't fire. There we had been guarding a power transformer all day and night with a useless gun."

Carl Illian, a chief electrician's mate on the *California,* told this story to his son shortly before he died in 1990.

"Even though it was Sunday morning, I had been up since shortly after

5 A.M. Sam, a shipmate and my close friend, decided that we should have breakfast and spend the day on the beach taking in the sights along with a few cold beers. We had finished breakfast and were enjoying a leisurely cup of coffee with a cigarette before heading back to our quarters.

"As we made our way topside, I made a comment to Sam about the vast temperature difference between Hawaii and what it surely must be like in my hometown of Midland, South Dakota. I clearly remember both of us laughing about the nonexistent chance of our enjoying a white Christmas in Honolulu, when suddenly we were startled by the sound of an explosion.

"As we continued on our way across the deck to try and determine where the sound had come from, we heard another explosion which appeared louder and closer than the first one. Suddenly there was the unmistakable sound of aircraft, and before we could come to grips with the reality of what was taking place, Sam and I were both thrown to the deck by the force of an onboard explosion. As I staggered to my feet, I recall seeing several small aircraft pass overhead, and to my amazement . . . they were not ours.

"We heard the sounding of General Quarters and immediately set out for our assigned stations. As I reached my station in the damage control center, I grabbed all three of the headsets and attempted to make contact with anyone I could. It was then that I realized from the conversation from the bridge that we were being attacked by Japanese aircraft.

"Within a few minutes a chief petty officer also assigned to the area appeared and asked me if I had any idea why they were holding drills on a Sunday morning. It was apparent that he had spent a considerable amount of the previous night in a local watering hole, and when I informed him of the seriousness of the situation, he responded by disappearing.

"The next thing I recall was hearing Sam's voice on one of the headsets, relaying to me the massive destruction of the after gyro control station where he was assigned. Since there was no need for him to remain there, I asked him to report to my station and give me some much-needed assistance. By now I was receiving more damage reports than I could possibly assess, and it was becoming increasingly difficult to respond to each report. Not until several days after the attack did I learn that my good friend Sam had become trapped in the after gyro station, which claimed his life.

"Information was being dispersed from areas throughout the ship which gave a clear indication that we were receiving extreme damage from the attack. Being confined to an area where I had no visual contact . . . made me realize my own peril, and I suddenly felt both fear and helplessness. It was about this time that the chief petty officer reappeared with several others who were assigned to the area. Due to our heavy list to the port side, I gave the order to transfer ballast to the starboard tanks, which helped remove the strain on the hawsers that were the only thing preventing us from capsizing.

"As the degree of list began to lessen, the order to abandon ship was given by the bridge command, which obviously meant the situation was hopeless. I reached the main deck, which was engulfed in heavy layers of smoke, and was again knocked from my feet by a severe explosion below deck. The explosions in and near the ship made movement difficult, and the burning oil in the water prevented us from diving overboard at that location. Bridge command was giving orders to abandon ship from the starboard bow, which provided the least dangerous swim to nearby Ford Island.

"We gathered in groups on the island and were assembled by ship identification, where a limited amount of first aid was given to those who needed it. Others who were able, were recruited on a volunteer basis to return to their ships to rescue survivors.

"Even though we had no way of knowing that the attack was over, I remember feeling no regard for my personal safety since it was apparent that men were trapped aboard the ship who desperately needed help. Once aboard the ship, several of us began cutting through the deck into the forward distribution station, where I knew several men would be trapped. After what seemed an eternity, we were able to extricate the division officer and five others. Their profound joy and relief was a heartwarming feeling that none of us would ever forget.

"We moved to the deck above the battery locker, where we cut off the ventilation housing air baffles and removed a portion of the deck that provided an opening large enough for the trapped man to escape, who was standing in water that had reached his chin."

Illian was largely responsible for the rescue of seven more men that day, and he received a captain's commendation and immediate promotion to chief electrician's mate.

Maurice Featherman was an ensign aboard the battleship *West Virginia*. He was barely awake when he heard the call "Away fire and rescue." Since he was the officer in charge of fire and rescue, he got up and began putting on his uniform. Then came the order to General Quarters, so he got out of his whites and into his dungarees, still not aware of the attack.

"As I made my way out of the junior officer bunk room, I saw a man running by, covered with fuel oil.

" 'Look what the bastards did to me,' he shouted.

"I was still very confused and thought to myself that if we were under attack, it must be by the Germans. But with what? How?"

Featherman's normal route to his battle station in the handling room of turret 4 was blocked because all watertight doors had been sealed, so he crossed to the other side of the ship, an act he thinks saved his life. He ended up in a compartment with about fifty men. Soon after, the ship was hit.

"I heard a series of loud explosions and breaking glass, then a very loud explosion nearby, and the lights went out. There was no panic among the men. Someone produced a flashlight, and by then the ship had a very acute list to port.

"The lights had been out for several minutes when I heard a series of bells which I believed to be the signal for abandoning ship. I was reassured when I heard that several of the men further aft had heard men shouting to abandon ship. Our whole group made our way forward, holding onto the outboard pipes on the bulkhead because of the severe list. I was in the rear, and it was a few minutes before I went through the first and only reopened watertight door on the way to the starboard quarterdeck hatch.

"I climbed up the ladder from the third deck and found men scrambling up the open cargo hatch to the quarterdeck, and the engineers were also coming up through a nearby hatch. I climbed up to the quarterdeck and found several men standing, watching the attack. I told them to cut down a life raft, and about three men got into it and the rest remained aboard the ship."

From the open quarterdeck, Featherman could see the destruction around him. Ahead of them the *Oklahoma* had capsized. Behind, the *Arizona* was sitting on the bottom, and what remained above the water was burning furiously. Across the harbor he saw the *Oglala* capsized, and the *California* was afire and sinking. His own ship was in a bad way, too.

"The *West Virginia* was on the bottom with her entire port side under water. Since my gun was under water, I went to turret 3, which was higher, and found it completely manned except for officers. I was sitting in the turret booth, legs dangling over, when suddenly there was a terrific shock. I saw flames shooting through cracks and holes in the bulkhead between gun rooms."

After trying to turn on sprinkling systems that did not work, Featherman dived into the water and started swimming with ten or fifteen men from the turret.

"I was tiring very quickly in the thick oil and water, so I made for a cushion floating nearby. I shared it with a sailor who was about to give up. A sailor with a life jacket came by and helped the one with me, so I made for a tug, which threw me a line and towed me about 100 yards before they pulled me aboard."

Elwood L. Whatley was a plane captain (now called flight engineer) in a PBY squadron stationed at Kaneohe Bay, the new seaplane base on the opposite side of Oahu from Pearl Harbor. For the past several weeks the planes had been going out on dawn patrol, three at 6 A.M. every day; they flew 300 miles out, made a 50-mile dogleg, then came back to the base.

"That morning my plane was the 'ready duty plane,' and it was at the head of the launch ramp some distance from the others, which were conveniently (for the Japanese) lined up wing tip to wing tip. The attacking aircraft merely flew a straight line, shooting at them. The Japs' method was to fire a small-caliber gun until they were sighted in and then cut in with their big guns, which carried incendiary ammunition. The result was total destruction of the aircraft.

"Since I was first in line, they got only a momentary shot at my plane, and all I got was bullet damage during the first attack. The second attack set the plane on fire, but we got it out before total destruction. As a result, the plane was later repaired and became known as the 'Flying Patch.'

"I was an eyewitness to the shooting down of the Zero piloted by Lieutenant Iida. I later went over to see where the plane had crashed and was somewhat surprised to see a Hamilton standard propeller, Zenith radio, and Goodyear tires.

"That night we established machine-gun nests around the base, especially in the bay area. During the night someone passed the word that Japanese paratroopers were landing and were wearing uniforms similar to ours.

"Someone issued orders and men were sent to the barracks to break into lockers, remove all white uniforms, and take them to the makeshift galley. There they were dumped into vats of coffee to disguise the white. Many men lost their clothing that way and many were running around in wet, coffee-dyed clothes.

"Then a little later a light was spotted on the dredge that was parked at Coconut Island, which was owned by the Fleischmann family. Apparently some men had been placed on the dredge, but the word didn't get out [to the rest of us]. So when the light was spotted on shore, the word went out that the Japanese had taken over the dredge, and our guns started firing. At the same time men on the dredge thought the Japanese had taken over the base and were attacking them, so they fired back. It was known as the Battle of the Dredge."

Harold S. Kaye was a radio operator with the 4th Reconnaissance Squadron of the 5th Bomber Group stationed at Hickam Field, and flew on B-17 Flying Fortresses. The following account is excerpted from an article he wrote for *Aerospace Historian.* Kaye was lying on his bunk when the attack started.

"A dull thud shook me out of a sound sleep and brought me up on one elbow. I looked around and noticed several men who were awakened by the same noise. Someone made the comment that it was a blasting noise made by the Navy and I laid my head back on the pillow when a sharp slamming noise accompanied by the tinkle of falling glass set me upright. Someone yelled, 'The Navy sure fouled up on that one!' I swung my legs out of the covers and dressed quickly, sticking my feet into non-regulation Indian moccasins and into my coveralls without undershirt or socks. While dressing I looked out the windows, which ran the length of the wall, and noticed a thick column of black smoke roiling up into the sky from the direction of Pearl Harbor.

"Downstairs I heard the first intimation that the planes were Japanese. Still, it didn't register. Some men were standing on the front steps and I went outside to join them. A low-flying plane came howling out of Pearl Harbor, thundered over the parade ground and roared past our barracks. The plane was a two-seater with a gunner in the rear cockpit and a fixed landing gear. Both pilot and gunner were helmeted and goggled and the rear gunner was frantically swiveling his machine gun from side to side. When I saw the large red balls painted on the underwing, I finally understood it was the Japanese.

"Over on the right of the steps, kneeling near some bushes, a soldier was firing a bolt-action Springfield rifle. Down the sidewalk toward the hangar I saw another airman flattening himself with his back to a palm tree as if to escape a slanting rain.

"At this point I witnessed an event that haunted me for years. For a long time I thought it might have been my imagination, but it was not: this same incident was seen by three other men.

"I saw a Japanese plane hit runway No. 3, sit there for a fraction of a second and then take off again. It was as if the Japanese pilot wanted to touch American soil and go back to his carrier with a good story.

"I thought it was safest to keep away from the entrance, so I went back inside. Every time a plane would roar past the barracks the airmen on the front steps and those crowded next to the entrance doors would come pelting back into the hallway. During one of those inrushes, I saw my first casualty. A tall soldier came walking in with blood on his forehead. It didn't look like a bullet wound, more like a cut from shattered glass or a flying stone.

"I was joined by my best friend, Stanley Foster, also a radio operator. We decided to sit down in a corridor next to the supply room with our backs to the wall. We hadn't been there long before the first sergeant of my outfit came into the hallway and yelled for crewmen attached to the planes, 'Get your ——— over to the flight line and help disperse the planes!'

"These were the first orders I heard that morning. The order guided me from aimless bewilderment to the sharp focus of duty. I trotted toward our squadron's hangar, No. 9, during a lull in the attack. I saw two men on a motorcycle motioning to an officer sitting in the pilot's seat of a B-17D parked on the flight line. They sped away and I spotted the number of the tail and it was the plane I had flown in with my commanding officer, Captain Louis P. Turner. The pilot saw me and waved to me to come over. As I ran toward the plane, the whine of the starter on the left outboard engine commenced with its accompanying cough and the prop turned over. Nearly to the plane, I recognized Lt. Gordon L. Kelley, who had been my copilot. He motioned me to come on board, the side door opened and the aerial engineer, Staff Sergeant Young, let down the stairs. I climbed aboard as the other engines coughed to life. When all were functioning, Kelley taxied the plane to a dispersal point next to the bomb dump.

"Our next task was to get the plane combat-ready because we had to start from scratch. There were no machine guns or ammunition in the planes and bombs had to be brought out from the bomb dump.

"Suddenly someone yelled, 'Get away from the plane; the Japs are attacking again!'

"We ran about 30 yards from the plane and stretched out on the ground. I propped myself up on one elbow. Looking out toward Pearl Harbor, I saw a Japanese plane pulling out of a dive, and as he emerged from the smoke, the plane disintegrated. I saw a throttled-back B-17E attempting to make a landing approach. Perhaps 50 yards behind him a Japanese fighter plane, with the leading edges of his wings winking furiously, was firing into the bomber. Either the pilot received instructions from the control tower or he realized what was happening because, with a sudden surge of power, the B-17E drew away from the Japanese fighter, made a climbing right turn over the ocean, and went back into his approach. The Japanese plane, which seemed to have been left standing still by the B-17E's sudden spurt of speed, made no attempt at another pass but continued on its way. Landing nicely after this trial, the pilot brought the B-17E to a stop off the runway and the crew spilled out in a hurry. I noticed the plane was painted a dull brown; ours were still silver-bright.

"PFC Lorenz, an airplane mechanic lying near us, shouted, 'Look up there!' I looked up and saw a V-shaped formation of 10 to 15 planes at about 8,000 feet, coming in from the ocean, flying east to west. Cottony-black balls of antiaircraft fire from Fort Kamehameha and Pearl Harbor exploded woefully short of their mark, at least 2,000 feet below the planes. A salvo of bombs was suddenly released. The sun caught the bombs as they fell, picking highlights here and there as they dropped.

"As the bombs struck, our barracks seemed to rise in the air and then settle back with dust and smoke piling up from the sides. The ground shook with the concussion. The bombs had landed on the west side of the barracks, but from the east wings my eye was caught by a rush of soldiers pouring out of the barracks like a disrupted anthill. Some were still in their underclothes or pajamas. . . .

"It seemed all clear again so we rejoined the plane and started the serious business of getting it combat-ready. Some progress already had been made, but the pace was maddeningly slow because of the confusion. The engineer, radio compartment, and rear bottom tub hatches were removed to be replaced with .50-caliber machine guns. A .30-caliber machine gun was positioned in the nose.

"Knowing I had to fly, I went back to the hangar on the tug to pick up my parachute. Hangar No. 9 was a mess, but not as badly damaged as the adjoining No. 7, which had been heavily bombed. All the clocks were stopped at 7:55. . . .

"Back at the plane . . . I snapped on the BC-348-B radio receiver and listened to the Hickam Field transmitting frequency. Nothing was coming in except background noise. . . .

"And then the most inspiring sight of the morning took place. A flight of three Douglas A-20 twin-engine bombers took off. Curiously, they took off from east to west. Almost invariably we took off in the opposite direction because of the winds which always seemed to come down off the Koolau Range.

"A force of three B-17D Flying Fortresses was assembled and taxied for takeoff on runway No. 3 going west to east. I watched [the first plane] through my radio compartment window pick up speed going down the runway, then suddenly veer off and come to a stop. The tail wheel had started to vibrate and the pilot told the copilot to lock the wheel, a standard procedure prior to takeoff, but the copilot mistakenly locked the elevators. The tail raised, ruining all four propellers. We came next and successfully took off the same runway.

"I cannot recall any fire coming our way but for days after the attack our plane had new holes every time we flew, from jittery gunners at Hickam, Pearl Harbor and Fort Kamehameha.

"Frankly I had no idea what direction we took in our pursuit of the Japanese carrier force. The thing I remember most about that flight was the cold; the bitter bone-aching cold. Apparently we had climbed to about 8,000 or 10,000 feet and stayed there a very long time. The combination of the altitude, plus the removal of the radio compartment's hatchway and my scanty attire, made for an uncomfortable ride. I know we reached 10,000 feet because Lt. Kelley came through and told me to put on my oxygen mask. Kelley came back through again and said I could take off my oxygen mask. Both times Kelley left the copilot seat he accidentally pulled the ripcord on his chutes and released them. Fortunately, however, he had 16 parachutes installed in the plane.

"Suddenly, in the twilight, we were preparing to land on runway No. 3. [Others in the crew] remember a large amount of incoming AA fire from our own land positions. In my isolated compartment, I had no knowledge of incoming fire. I remember an uneventful landing and then swinging off the concrete runway and onto the field. Cold and weary, I climbed stiffly out of our plane. We were surrounded by a large group of men. And now I felt the first glow of pride and heroism as the men gathered around us and spoke in admiring ways. 'Did you see anything?' someone asked. 'No,' I answered, 'I didn't see a thing.'

"Someone from our crew asked if we could find something to eat. I hadn't eaten since 6 P.M. the previous night. The enlisted men were told that Hickam Hospital had the only hot food so we made our way there. Inside, the hospital was dimly lit and blankets were draped over the windows for blackout purposes. Apparently families had been evacuated from their homes and were lodged in the hospital. Children were crying and women were talking in anxious voices. Others were lying quietly on mattresses on the floor. It looked and sounded like a somber movie setting.

"We ate some lukewarm stew and then walked back to the Hangar No. 9 operations room. A hot rumor awaited our arrival. Japanese gliders were going to land! I went outside and looked up at the sky. Scudding clouds were passing below the stars and with a stretched imagination one could visualize moving lights. All around the field men had set up improvised machine gun nests for AA protection. These men were extremely trigger-happy; every time a tug would start up or a strange noise occurred, someone would stutter their machine gun, arcing tracers into the dark sky.

"I was ordered to be on the flight line at 4:30 A.M. and to report to my plane for another mission. We were also told where to sleep. I found myself in a NCO's home lying on a mattress placed on the floor, listening to a telephone conversation between a Master Sergeant and his wife, who had been evacuated to Honolulu. The Master Sergeant was trying to placate his wife and the conversation droned on and on. The shock of the attack and subsequent events had worn off and I began worrying about the takeoff the next morning. I began to feel my first fear of the day. Sleeping would be difficult."

John Garcia was a sixteen-year-old shipfitter's apprentice at Pearl Harbor when the attack came. His grandmother shook him awake and told him of the attack, and that all military and civilian personnel were supposed to report. Garcia got dressed and jumped on his bicycle to pedal the four miles to Pearl Harbor, still not quite believing it was not realistic maneuvers.

He arrived during a lull in the attack and was able to get his tools. When the Japanese planes returned, Garcia took cover beneath concrete steps and watched as the *Pennsylvania* was hit and the destroyers *Cassin* and *Downes* were blown up. He had been working on the *Pennsylvania* and knew the ship well, so when he was ordered aboard it to help put out fires on the marine deck, he refused.

"I had been working next to the marine deck and knew that this was where the powder for the big guns was stored. If the fire hit there, the ship would be cut in half.

"Then they told me to go into the water and help rescue sailors who had been blown off or jumped off the ships. I saw less danger in that, and some other men and I started pulling people out. Many were alive but stunned and disoriented, and of course many were dead. The ocean was on fire with oil, but I had plenty of practice swimming in burning oil from a water-safety project I had been on when I worked for Pan Am.

"That afternoon I punched out and started home, but I found the gate to the base locked and was told nobody could go home. We were to report back to whatever ship we had been working on, if it was still there. So I went back to the *Pennsylvania.* The fires were out now, and the powder had been removed.

"Around midnight I went up on deck for a break and heard some machine-gun fire. I found out later that someone working on the armor plate of the ship had lit a cigarette, and some Marines nearby thought it was a signal to the Japanese and opened fire.

"Later that night I was called on to drive a truckload of Marines up to Palolo Valley, about twenty-five miles from Pearl Harbor, because there had been a report that some Japanese paratroopers landed there. They chose me because I knew the island well and could drive in the dark. We didn't smash into anything, and when we got there, Marines scattered all over the area, yelling into their radios to base twenty-five miles away. The radios had a range of about five miles.

"Someone on the ridge heard the noise and turned on the porch light. The Marines began firing at him or the light, and the light went out. They were shooting about 1,000 yards up the ridge, and I don't think the bullets even got up there.

"At dawn they checked the whole valley, and there were no paratroopers. We went back to the base, but not before stopping along the way for breakfast.

"I went back to the shipfitters' shop to find my next job, and we got word that tapping was being heard from the keel of the USS *West Virginia.* We armed ourselves with blowtorches and pneumatic hammers and took a launch out to the ship. The *West Virginia* had been blown upside down, and the keel was sticking out of the water.

"We couldn't use the blowtorches because there might have been gases . . . so we had to use the slow process of using the hammers to cut the rivets on the plates. As soon as we got the plates off, a number of sailors came rushing out of there, knocking some of us into the water. Again I had to go into the water because some of the guys that were knocked into the water had tool belts on and were weighted down with heavy tools. No one died and no one was hurt. And those sailors had been at the bottom of the ship for eighteen hours."

Not all *West Virginia* sailors were so lucky; three remained trapped alive until Christmas Eve.

3

Adventures of the *Henley*

At about the time Outerbridge was firing the first shots of the war, two privates, Joseph Lockard and George Elliott, were manning the Army's Opana radar station on Kahuku Point, the most northerly point on Oahu. Radar was not sophisticated at the time, and the station was operated only a few hours a day. After General Short received a "war warning" from Washington on November 27, he had ordered that the radar station be operated daily from 4 A.M. to 7 A.M.

When 7 A.M. came, Lockard and Elliott were supposed to shut it down and an Army truck would pick them up for breakfast. The truck was late, so the privates kept the radar on and Lockard was teaching Elliott how the equipment worked. At 7:02 Elliott saw a large blob on the screen and called to Lockard. He recognized it as a fleet of planes and computed them to be approaching from 3 degrees north and 136 miles away, a long distance for the primitive radar to pick up.

Elliott was startled by the size of the blip and guessed it would be caused by at least fifty planes. He and Lockard followed it for a few moments, then Elliott suggested that Lockard call it into the information center.

The station had two telephones, one to the information center and the other to the administrative switchboard. They tried the information center line first but nobody answered, so they tried the administrative telephone operator, who told them he was the only one there. The operator hung up, looked around, and saw that Lieutenant Kermit Tyler, the pursuit duty officer, was still there, so he told the lieutenant about the radar sighting. The lieutenant told him to call the radar operators and tell them to forget it; it had to be the fleet of B-17 bombers coming in that morning from the mainland.

When the operator called the Opana station, Lockard answered, more excited than before. He demanded to speak to an officer, so Tyler took the phone, listened to his story, told him to forget about it, and hung up. The privates shrugged and went outside to wait for the truck that would take them to breakfast, taking the station log with them to show their friends at the base. Nobody had ever seen such a large fleet of planes in the Hawaiian Islands.

While the *Ward* was getting the war off to a good start, another destroyer was in a state of confusion. The *Henley* had been out the previous week on fleet maneuvers with two battleships. The battleships were supposed to be firing their antiaircraft guns, but they did not fire a round; instead, the ships were kept busy searching for unidentified submarines their sonar operators reported. The ships came in on Friday, December 5, and the *Henley* returned to its mooring buoy north of Ford Island with two other destroyers, the *Ralph Talbot* and the *Patterson.* The *Henley* was moored on the outside, toward the channel entrance.

Most of the senior officers were ashore, along with two-thirds of the crew, leaving only junior officers and a skeleton crew aboard. Officer of the deck was a reserve ensign named Joseph A. Groden.

"I had the officer of the deck watch from noon Saturday until noon Sunday and had made my proper rounds about midnight, then finished a game of checkers with a signalman before turning in at 0330," Groden said. "I planned to get up about 0800.

"About 0730 I heard the General Alarm gong.

"I raced down to the quarterdeck in my shoes, a pair of pants and a T-shirt, yelling, 'What's going on?' Everybody was racing around to their battle stations.

"The petty officer of the deck was Don Wilson, a torpedoman third class. He was a hell of a humorous guy, one of the funniest men I've ever known, and he was the one who caused it [the confusion]. He came up early to relieve the 0400 to 0800 watch—he was supposed to be on from 0800 until noon—and he was laughing and joking around as usual, and he reached behind him without looking to hit the gas alarm five times to call the Muster to Stations alarm, to get the crew out of bed.

"He wasn't paying attention, and he hit the General Quarters alarm. When you hit it, there's no turning back. It is automatic and it makes a terrible racket. So everybody jumped out of the sack and raced to their battle stations. The engineers had to light off the boilers, the engines had to be turned over and the ammunition brought up to the handling rooms for the big guns."

Wilson confirms Groden's version, adding that he had been up since 0400 because the ordnancemen were going to remove two exercise heads from torpedoes and replace them with warheads.

"A few minutes before 0800 the chief asked me if I didn't have the 0800–1200 watch, and told me to go get cleaned up and into my dress whites," he said. "I cleaned up and put on my whites, and since I was almost late, ran down to the galley and got an egg sandwich. Then I went up to relieve the watch.

"While the petty officer was telling me everything that had been going on, I bit into the sandwich and soft egg yolk ran down my chin and on my white uniform. I cursed. At the same time the messenger on deck said it was 0755, time to sound the alarm calling the crew to muster.

"I was still complaining and trying to wipe off the egg, and without looking, reached behind me and hit the wrong one. Lieutenant (j.g.) Fleck came out and asked what was going on, and I told him.

" 'Well, just yell down to belay it,' he said, so I told the messenger to go down to the galley and I would go down to the crew's quarters.

"I was kind of a loose wire anyway, and things didn't bother me. I went down to tell the crew, and when I got back to the afterdeck, a shipfitter named Erickson was sitting on a ready ammunition locker and a big explosion went up on Ford Island, so I ran back to the quarterdeck."

Groden, the officer of the deck, was waiting for him.

"By the time I got to the bridge, I was berating Wilson for his carelessness and suggested that maybe he'd better not pick up his liberty card for three weeks," Groden said. "We could do that rather than putting a man on report and going before the mast and getting it on his service record.

"While we were standing there and I was trying to get everything squared away and back to normal so we could cancel General Quarters, a Japanese torpedo plane flew by at eye level, right alongside our ship, and dropped a torpedo that went across the harbor into the USS *Utah* that was tied up alongside Ford Island.

"I looked at Wilson. Wilson looked at me. For an instant we couldn't figure out what was happening, but in the distance we saw all the explosions, the USS *Arizona* blowing up and all that, and then we had a message from Commander in Chief, U.S. Fleet, saying 'Japanese air attack on Pearl Harbor. This is no drill.'

"By the time the message came, we had already figured it out and were getting under way. Lieutenant Fleck was a fabulous young officer, and he later became a rear admiral. He was an Academy graduate while the rest of us were reserves. He was the senior officer aboard and he took over. Thanks to Wilson, the boilers were already lighted and the engines were turning over, so we hacked off the mooring lines and left."

It was almost exactly 8:30 when they pulled away from the other destroyers and headed for the open sea. At that moment the ship's skipper was some distance away in a motor whaleboat, watching his ship head off to war.

"Out on the stern we had a canvas awning over the fantail to cover the men while we showed movies, and the chief bosun's mate wanted to take the time to unlash it and stow it away, which would have been a laborious process," Groden said. "The chief gunner's mate said he'd take care of it. He put a 'bale of hay,' which is a powder case on a five-inch gun without a projectile, into the number 4 gun and fired it into the canopy. It blew out a big blast of black smoke, steam, and hot air, and all it left of the canopy was some smoking shreds of canvas.

"We were the second ship out of the harbor. The USS *Helm* beat us because they were already under way over near the entrance to the harbor at the West Block, running some degaussing [hull demagnatizing] tests.

"We shot down a couple of Japanese planes. Unfortunately, we also shot down an American fighter that was . . . coming in with the guard mail. We got him with a five-inch shell, and he never knew what hit him. We also shot at the B-17s that were high overhead. We missed them by thousands of feet, but nobody had ever seen the B-17s before, and since they were strange, we naturally assumed they were Japanese."

In the meantime, the senior officers of the *Henley* were having their own problems. The skipper, Lieutenant Commander Robert Hall Smith, and the executive officer, Lieutenant H. G. "Steve" Corey, lived near each other. Corey was awakened that morning by the sound of gunfire and explosions, and he turned on the radio to see what was happening. The announcer said that all military personnel were ordered back to their stations, and then the station went back to playing music as normal.

Smith and Corey had arranged to keep their whaleboat at the Aiea landing, at the far northeastern end of Pearl Harbor, assuming that in case of an emergency they would not be able to get through the confusion at the fleet landing.

When they talked on the phone, Smith said he would drive; he picked up Corey, and they raced to the Aiea parking lot. He tossed his car keys to the attendant, saying his wife would pick them up later, and sprinted to the dock. When they ran toward the whaleboat, the Hawaiian woman who operated a hot dog stand at the landing pointed a rifle at them and shouted, "Halt!" They skidded to a stop and spent precious moments convincing her of their identity, then took off to the whaleboat, where the ship's engineer and whaleboat coxswain were already waiting.

They headed out into the bay, feeling very vulnerable in the open boat, making their way through the smoke, bullets, bombs, and total confusion. At last they spotted their ship, but to their dismay the *Henley* was steaming for the open ocean, bow up and throwing a heavy wake, stern almost submerged, and men at their battle stations. Smith was hopping mad and would later make Fleck's life miserable for leaving him behind, although Fleck was doing what Navy regulations required in such a situation.

"Our instructions were absolutely clear on this count," Groden said. "In case of attack, we were to get the hell out of Pearl Harbor and head for the open sea. Fleck did exactly the right thing, and it ate at him for all those years that he had handled the situation superbly, exactly by the book, and he got chewed out for it. In fact, he didn't even receive a commendation for his actions that day, while other men who did less received them. I assume it was because Smith had put a reprimand in his record. I've often thought those of us aboard the ship that day should try to have that situation rectified in Washington."

Wilson agrees. He said that years later, during one of the *Henley* reunions, Mrs. Fleck asked him to be her dinner partner. ("Talk about sagebrush and palm trees!" Wilson said.) She told him that her husband had always been hurt by not being recognized for his actions that day.

The *Henley* cleared the harbor without being hit and got out to sea while Smith and Corey kept up the chase. They caught up with the *Selfridge,* the destroyer that was their squadron flagship; but when they found it was not going to sea, they took off through the explosions and rain of shrapnel in search of a more suitable ship.

While they were racing around the harbor in the whaleboat, American antiaircraft batteries went into operation, and shrapnel from them, plus that from Japanese bombs and exploding ships, filled the air with pieces of flying metal. Smith, Corey, and the other two men did the only thing they could: They covered their heads with the whaleboat's seat cushions. They would have been no more help than a helmet of palm fronds, but they felt good at the time. It also gave them a good laugh when it was over.

Finally, at almost ten o'clock, after the last attack was over and the sky began clearing of smoke, they pulled alongside a destroyer-turned-minesweeper, the *Trever,* a ship about as old as the *Ward.* They were told the ship was headed out to sea, so they abandoned the whaleboat and went to sea on antisubmarine patrol. They soon came within sight of the *Henley,* but the temporary skipper of the *Trever* would not let them borrow the ship's whaleboat. He said he was saving it in case his skipper showed up and needed it for transfer—and indeed the skipper did show up late that afternoon.

Smith and Corey were determined to get aboard their ship, so when the *Trever* got near it, they decided to swim across. They did not want to lose their wallets and identification, so rather than stripping down to their skivvies, they cut off their trouser legs at the knee, took off their shoes and socks, dived into the ocean, and began paddling toward the *Henley.* They struggled for a while, but the current kept separating them from the destroyer; they had to give up and go back on board the *Trever.* Finally, about noon they tried again. The *Henley* went into a tight port turn to create a "slick," a smooth spot in the sea. The crew tossed over a life raft; the officers climbed into it and were pulled across to their ship.

Once on board, Smith relieved Fleck of command and went looking for his favorite stool to sit on and relax after a hectic morning. He could not find it and asked the bridge crew where they had put it. A seaman said he had thrown it over the side. Smith was momentarily speechless. He had chased his ship through an air raid with bombs, bullets, and torpedoes all around him; had watched much of the American fleet sinking; had hitched rides on ships; had tried to swim in the open ocean; had bobbed between two ships in a life raft—and now his favorite stool was gone because a lowly seaman had thrown it overboard. He finally found his voice and asked why he had done that.

"Because it was made of wood and wood's inflammable," the seaman replied with irrefutable logic, referring to naval regulations regarding combat readiness. It was one of the low points of Smith's day.

4

Game Called Due to War

One of the more unusual experiences was that of two mainland college football teams who were in Honolulu for postseason games at the University of Hawaii. San Jose State College and Willamette University, a private university in Salem, Oregon, had sent their football teams to play two games in Honolulu between Thanksgiving and Christmas. Each mainland team would play the University of Hawaii, then they would play each other.

It was strictly a pleasure trip: The games were an excuse to go on a luxurious ship to Hawaii, tour the island, chase girls, and in general have a good time before Christmas. It would be the last fling as civilians for several seniors because they had received notices from the draft board that they were classified 1-A and were to report for induction right after Christmas. Indeed, several of the Californians had been given short deferments in order to make the trip.

The trip was not an annual event for either team, but it had been made by the California team in the past, in part because a former San Jose State player, Dick Hubbel, was now a Honolulu policeman. Born and reared in Hawaii, Hubbel had remained active in alumni affairs.

The Willamette-Hawaii game was played Saturday, December 6, and the Hawaiians won by 20 to 6. The San Jose State team was scheduled to play the Hawaiians on December 10; three days later the mainland teams would play each other and leave for home so they would be there for Christmas.

The trip was almost called off. Not long before their scheduled departure on December 1, the teams were told the trip was canceled because of the tense situation with Japan. A few days later they were told the situation had improved and the trip would be made as planned.

The teams traveled on the Matson liner *Lurline.* A large group of students, friends, and boosters accompanied the Willamette team. The San Jose athletes came from families of more modest incomes, and most of the players were traveling alone. An exception was a recently married player whose wife was along.

This economic gap, plus the sports rivalry, kept the players from associating much with each other on the ship and in the hotel. Even after the attack they went their own ways and friendships did not develop.

"How we ate on the ship," said Chet Carsten, the San Jose fullback. "We could have as much of anything as we wanted—a whole pie if we wanted, everything. We all gained about ten pounds on the way over and had to have extra workouts to get back in shape."

The teams received a royal welcome when they landed at the commercial pier near the center of Honolulu. One of the girls accompanying the Willamette team was engaged to a Navy pilot, and he got permission for his squadron to fly over the *Lurline* when it entered the harbor. The ship was met by the usual Hawaiian band with singers and hula dancers, and the lovely girls waiting at the foot of the gangway with leis and gentle cheek kisses. Both teams stayed in the Ala Moana Hotel on Waikiki Beach, a U-shaped palace to the students that "now looks like a cabin among the high-rises," Carsten said.

That Sunday morning both teams were scheduled to go on trips around the island. The University of Hawaii, represented by several campus beauties, was taking the California boys; a feast of chicken, fruit, gallons of pineapple juice, and vegetables was delivered to the hotel. The Oregonians were going to be escorted around the island by the local Shriners. The teams had breakfast and were sitting in the dining room when Dick Hubbel came in and told them the island trip was off because Japan had attacked Pearl Harbor. Every vehicle on the island was being used, and the rumors were already rampant that the Japanese had landed on the windward side and that their paratroopers were already in the mountains and were on their way to Honolulu.

Everyone dashed to the hotel roof to watch the show, but Pearl Harbor is about fifteen miles from Waikiki and they could not see or hear very much. They were startled, though, by two or three American antiaircraft shells that landed in the street nearby and "made salt and pepper shakers out of some houses," Carsten said.

There was not much for the young athletes to do, so most simply sat around for the rest of Sunday and through the night made longer by the blackout. The California contingent took the picnic food down the street to Kuhio Park and had a feast "rather than let it go to waste."

The next day the *Lurline* left for the mainland, and nobody knew if they would ever see it again. Before panic or complete boredom set in, they decided to join the war effort. The Willamette students were assigned to the Punahou School, which was being used as a supply depot.

The San Jose students also got busy, and several went down to the police station to see their friend Dick Hubbel. They volunteered because, Carsten said, they wanted to "get ahold of something that would shoot." He suggested police work to the San Jose coach, Ben Winkleman, so Winkleman and several others marched down to the Honolulu Police Station. There was such a shortage of policemen in Honolulu that the students were issued riot guns, arm bands, helmets and gas masks; they patrolled with the regular policemen for about a week.

Soon the volunteers' numbers dwindled, and in a few days eight California students determined to be policemen were going to police school eight hours during the day and patrolling at night. They assumed they would be drafted but also believed that having the police experience would improve their military career. All preferred being military policemen to being infantrymen.

Few had any money, and that was an immediate concern of Jack Hedgecock, a Willamette student who had spent nearly all his money on the ticket over. The morning after the attack he went downtown and started job hunting. The first place he walked in had only Oriental clerks, which he was unaccustomed to, and they stood around listening while he talked to the owner, a Caucasian. Hedgecock remembers him as looking nonplussed when he asked for a job. He did not get a job that day.

However, it worked out well for Hedgecock because the Army paid the students a nominal amount for guarding the school and gave them infantry food; several of them were able to pool their resources and rent one room in the Ala Moana to use for showers and clothing storage. They, too, were issued rifles and at first stood four-hours-on, four-hours-off watches at the school, but that became so exhausting that they changed it to four hours on and eight hours off.

The coaching staff got a message back to Oregon that the Willamette students were in good health, and the governor of Oregon, Charles A. Sprague, called the students' parents to reassure them that their children were safe and would be home soon.

On the way over, the San Jose students had befriended a steel company representative named Stan Cronin, and he let seven of them sleep on his hotel-room floor and couches, then loaned them $200, which the young policemen used to rent a house in Kaimuki where "the beds were always hot because we all worked different shifts," Carsten said.

The students made it home for Christmas, many arriving on Christmas Day. Carsten said they were told two hours before the ship left that they were going home. He was one who did not return. "They offered us a job on the police force," Carsten said, "and seven of us took their offer. When we were told we had two hours to leave, the eighth took off for home without even getting his paycheck from the police department."

Carsten had gotten engaged to his college sweetheart; six months later his fiancée moved to Honolulu, and they were married. He was one of the few who stayed on the Honolulu police force throughout the war, in part because he was married and soon had a child. He says he ran a USO for everyone he knew from California who came through Hawaii during the war, and it was not unusual for him and his wife to have five or six guests for dinner. One Christmas they had fourteen friends from home with them.

One tragedy occurred. One of the seven who stayed, Bill Donnelly, died of a ruptured appendix about five months after the attack. "Having to call his parents was one of the hardest things I've ever done," Carsten said.

Most left Hawaii after the war and returned to the mainland, and four or five of them went into coaching. Paul Pognetti, the San Jose quarter-back, remained in Honolulu and married a local girl. They had twin daughters; one was elected Miss Teen Hawaii and the other one was the runner-up.

Even though the war interfered with their college education, San Jose State made no allowances for the team members. "We had to go back after the war and take all the courses over again that we had dropped in December 1941," Carsten said. "Even a swimming class in PE."

ent from the Koolau Range. It was a hard hike going up, during which went up about 1,500 feet, and got to the top at 2,700 feet. At odd ervals on the way up we would hear the guns firing again, and we uld listen for the shells, but none came.

"We spent the whole day there, collecting plants and looking at things w to us. From the peak we could see all over the island. Wheeler and rl Harbor were still burning, and it was then that I became certain nething had happened to Pearl Harbor because the smoke coming from was a dense black, and I was sure it was oil smoke, though I still ught it was an accident.

'The trip down was uneventful. I was worn out when we got back to cars at about 5:30. The sun was beginning to go down by the time we ted home.

'It got dark before we reached Pearl Harbor and we turned on our its, although everybody else was driving with blue lights, if they had on at all. Army trucks were tearing by in both directions, passing us both sides, which made Mrs. Richardson quite angry; we had a five-iute tirade on the recklessness of the Army truck drivers, all the acci-ts they were responsible for, etc.

When we came to the rotary where our road joined the Pearl Harbor l, five or six military police were standing there, but none said any-g about our lights. We drove on until we reached Red Hill, near Pearl bor but above it, and stopped to look at the blaze on Ford Island it a mile away. It was on the same dock I had worked on when I came to Hawaii in September.

A mile further on, several Boy Scouts stopped us and ordered us to out our lights. When we asked why, they said simply, 'Japan has ked us,' and in a flash the whole thing became clear to us. All the es, all the bombing, all the shooting, all the fires we had seen that ning had been due to the Japanese.

After we turned out our car lights, it was so dark that Dr. Richardson dn't see to drive, so I got out and dogtrotted along the curb for the mile so that he could follow my white shirt and stay on the road. It rather frightening getting there. All the houses were dark and no s on the street, until suddenly a military policeman would flash a and stop us, inspect us and let us go. It seemed as though it must be in the morning, but when I realized it was only about 7:30 in the ing, it made me think I was in a city of the dead.

The first people we talked to were neighbors of the Richardsons, who over as soon as we arrived. They told us that the Japs had demol-

5

View from the Cane Fields

Alan Conger arrived in Honolulu in September 1941 to begin graduate school at the University of Hawaii. He kept a detailed diary, and the following story was taken from an account of the attack he wrote on December 8. Like many who witnessed the attack, he now finds it hard to believe how naive he and his companions were.

On that Sunday morning Conger went on a field trip with his taxonomy class into the Wainai Mountains. He was picked up at 6:30 by a Honolulu dentist named Richardson and his wife, who were friends and admirers of the professor, Dr. Harold St. John. St. John permitted several nonstudents to accompany his classes on the outings, in part because they helped provide transportation for the students.

Conger and the Richardsons went to Waipahu to meet the rest of the group of about ten. Their route took them past Pearl Harbor and Schofield Barracks before the servicemen were stirring.

"About three miles south of Schofield, we turned west and started driving through the pineapple fields to get up to the edge of the mountains, where we would start hiking," Conger said. "It was while we were driving through the open pineapple fields that we began to notice things happening. We were about three miles from Schofield and about two and a half miles from Wheeler Field, and about 900 feet above them.

"I noticed planes diving down on Wheeler Field, and wanted to watch, so all of us stopped and got out [of the cars] to watch the show. It was a thrilling sight: Planes could be heard flying above the clouds which hid them from sight. Then you could hear their engines begin to scream as they started to dive, drop straight down on Wheeler Field, drop their bombs and fly by. Of course none of us knew that this was the real thing. The Army and Navy had been on the alert for five days, and Dr. St. John and Dr. Richardson, both of whom had been there several years and were accustomed to those things, assured me, the newcomer of the party, that it was merely part of the practice maneuvers.

"I counted fifteen planes dropping out of the clouds and leaving their bombs on Wheeler Field, but do not know how many had already descended before we got out to watch. What amazed me, though, was that the planes were dropping real bombs. Four times, as a plane leveled out over the field, I could actually see the bombs fall out of the planes and drop to the earth, and see the big explosion and the smoke they caused, and a few seconds later feel the earth shake under me, and the air push against me like a heavy wave.

"By this time Wheeler was obscured in smoke and dust, but those planes which had already dropped their bombs circled back and began strafing the ground. We could hear their machine guns fire, and see some of them flying into the smoke over the field, not more than fifty feet above it. I was still incredulous because I could see that the planes were bombing the field itself, and things were burning, and I couldn't believe it was nothing more than practice. However, the people who had lived there, which included everyone but Lois Eubank, another graduate student, and me, said it must be practice. I am sure everyone must have considered the possibility that it was a real attack, for we spoke about it and asked one another what it would be like if it were Japan attacking. How innocent we were."

Three of Dr. St. John's four children, two sons and one daughter, were on the hike. Mary, then ten years old, said that when they saw things exploding, the adults were totally convinced that the Army was holding maneuvers because the newspapers had carried stories alerting civilians that war games would be played on the island. They assumed the first big explosion they saw was "some noodlehead dropping a bomb on the Standard Oil of California tanks by mistake."

Conger was fascinated. "Several planes flew right above us, and I remember looking at them and noticing that they were U.S. planes, for I could see the markings on their rudders, of the type they were using in 1935 or thereabouts and were then using for training pilots after they had graduated from primary training. One group of three pursuit planes flew over, but they were going too fast and I wouldn't have thought of looking at their markings anyway.

"By this time the planes had ceased diving and dro
on Wheeler Field and were scurrying around practici
so we thought, so we got back in our cars and drove
further through the fields toward the mountains."

Then the group almost became one of the frien
American shells began falling to earth near them.

"As we were driving, we noticed that the shells wer
on the field where we were, which did scare us exceed
me. We stopped, got out to look around, and were
more shells were dropping in the field. It was then
maneuvers had moved down to Pearl Harbor, whi
miles from us. We could see planes there, as small s
the bomb explosions on Ford Island and all around I

"And still we thought it was practice. The battles
in Pearl Harbor were firing like mad; there were hu
bursts over the harbor, but it was too far away for u
planes were hit. We could see smoke coming up fr
very plainly could see flashes from guns on the ships

"About this time more shells began plopping into
Two landed within a hundred yards of us and e
shrapnel hit us. The terrifying thing was that we
coming, and didn't know when one would hit us. T
wobbly whistle in the air, which would gradually go
shell came nearer, and soon it would land and exp
that my heart was in my mouth and I was scared
don't believe more than ten shells landed near us, b

"As soon as the shells stopped coming, everyo
about the whole thing and Mrs. Richardson, wh
admiral or something at Pearl Harbor, said she w
hell the next morning for firing the guns up in t
any announcement in the paper or radio.

"We again turned toward Pearl Harbor, and e
the guns fire, I quaked in my boots while waiti
shell, but no more came our way. Smoke was
Island, which obscured much of the harbor, but
ships firing and shells bursting in the air. Wheele
hind a great cloud of smoke and seemed to have
"Shortly after the shells stopped landing, we d
to the edge of the field and began our hike up int
the first time I had been in the Wainais, and the

ished every airfield on the island: Wheeler, Hickam, Kaneohe, Pearl Harbor, Belling, and that hardly a plane had been able to get off the ground. All the ships had been trapped in Pearl Harbor and had tried to get out into the sea.

"After more exchange of news, we went into the Richardsons' house, stumbled around in the dark, tried to hang rugs, curtains, and blankets over the windows, but were unable to black out anything but the kitchen. Mrs. Richardson made some soup for us, the only thing she could prepare. I had Campbell's onion soup, a trivial detail but I had only a small can of cold baked beans and was hungry as a bear, and a glass of port. The food made us all feel better.

"I called Louisa Palmer, a friend of my mother who was teaching at the university, because she was the only person in Hawaii who might have wondered about me.

"Lois and I left at about 8:30, and Mrs. Richardson said that she imagined we would never forget each other after the experience of spending the first day of the war together. I thought she was right.

"Lois and I walked about two miles home. It was dark and raining by this time, and occasionally a star would peek through a hole in the clouds. The streets were practically deserted, the only indication of life being an occasional flash of light from a soldier on guard on a street corner.

"I felt extremely depressed and down in the dumps. I didn't feel any resentment or anger against anyone. The whole affair made me so sad I could have wept. It is impossible that the world population wants anything like this. As we walked up Manoa Road, which goes up Punahou Hill behind Punahou School, I was impressed with the darkness of the city spread out below, from Diamond Head to Pearl Harbor.

"We got to Lois's without incident, and her sister was in when we arrived, her ear glued to her radio. From there I went to see Louisa, and she had sent some cablegrams that morning. I asked her to send one home for me saying, 'Safe. Tell Pris.' Pris was Priscilla Nash, who four years later became my wife.

"Then I toddled home through the dark and was stopped by some American Legionnaires on duty at the corner of Oahu and Kamehameha, chatted with them for a minute and went on home."

The St. John family had an equally exciting evening.

"My father was always the last to leave because he wanted to be sure everyone was accounted for when we left the mountains," Mary St. John Zemach said. "By the time we left, it was getting dark and we had the car lights on.

"My brother Charles had just got his driver's license and was driving, and we started off down the highway, which at that time had three lanes, two regular lanes and a center lane for passing. We hadn't gone far until a motorcycle came up behind us and the man shouted, 'Watch your lights, buddy!' We didn't know what the problem was. Someone thought perhaps he meant Charles should turn the beam up, so he did.

"Shortly after that we were stopped by a policeman. He looked inside the car and said, 'My God, it's Dr. St. John.' He was a former botany student, and he knew instantly what we were doing and why we hadn't heard anything. He told us we were at war and said he was supposed to make all civilians spend the night beside the road, but since he knew my father, he had us follow him to the Pearl City police station to have our lights painted over.

"My father took over the driving and drove down the middle lane with no lights on, and it was one of the scariest rides I've ever been on. We got to Pearl City alive and someone painted out our lights with a rolled-up newspaper dipped in dark blue ink. . . .

"Then they told us we could try to get to Honolulu but there was no guarantee we could make it. The policeman warned us to use the lights as little as possible because some civilians were shooting at headlights. So we took off again. There was no moon but just enough light from the stars to see a little. To make it worse for us, most streets in those days were covered by large trees. . . . So it was really difficult.

"Every time we blinked on the lights to see where we were, people shouted at us, and we assumed they were trigger-happy people.

"We got home and rolled into the driveway and my mother rushed out, peered into the car to count heads, and without saying anything else, said, 'Harold, there's a Navy wife in the basement with a loaded revolver. Would you please take it away from her?'

"She and my little sister, who was eight, had stayed home because it was a long hike, too long for my sister, who wasn't a strong hiker yet. They had started to walk to church—we didn't have a radio because my father disapproved of them—so she didn't know what had happened. They hadn't gone very far before an elderly woman rushed out onto her porch and said, 'Mrs. St. John, you must get off the street immediately!'

"My mother thought, 'Oh dear, Mrs. ——— has finally gone over the edge.'

" 'It's all right,' mother told her. 'We're just going to church.'

"The woman was insistent, so my mother and sister went into the

5

View from the Cane Fields

Alan Conger arrived in Honolulu in September 1941 to begin graduate school at the University of Hawaii. He kept a detailed diary, and the following story was taken from an account of the attack he wrote on December 8. Like many who witnessed the attack, he now finds it hard to believe how naive he and his companions were.

On that Sunday morning Conger went on a field trip with his taxonomy class into the Wainai Mountains. He was picked up at 6:30 by a Honolulu dentist named Richardson and his wife, who were friends and admirers of the professor, Dr. Harold St. John. St. John permitted several nonstudents to accompany his classes on the outings, in part because they helped provide transportation for the students.

Conger and the Richardsons went to Waipahu to meet the rest of the group of about ten. Their route took them past Pearl Harbor and Schofield Barracks before the servicemen were stirring.

"About three miles south of Schofield, we turned west and started driving through the pineapple fields to get up to the edge of the mountains, where we would start hiking," Conger said. "It was while we were driving through the open pineapple fields that we began to notice things happening. We were about three miles from Schofield and about two and a half miles from Wheeler Field, and about 900 feet above them.

"I noticed planes diving down on Wheeler Field, and wanted to watch, so all of us stopped and got out [of the cars] to watch the show. It was a thrilling sight: Planes could be heard flying above the clouds which hid them from sight. Then you could hear their engines begin to scream as they started to dive, drop straight down on Wheeler Field, drop their bombs and fly by. Of course none of us knew that this was the real thing. The Army and Navy had been on the alert for five days, and Dr. St. John and Dr. Richardson, both of whom had been there several years and were accustomed to those things, assured me, the newcomer of the party, that it was merely part of the practice maneuvers.

"I counted fifteen planes dropping out of the clouds and leaving their bombs on Wheeler Field, but do not know how many had already descended before we got out to watch. What amazed me, though, was that the planes were dropping real bombs. Four times, as a plane leveled out over the field, I could actually see the bombs fall out of the planes and drop to the earth, and see the big explosion and the smoke they caused, and a few seconds later feel the earth shake under me, and the air push against me like a heavy wave.

"By this time Wheeler was obscured in smoke and dust, but those planes which had already dropped their bombs circled back and began strafing the ground. We could hear their machine guns fire, and see some of them flying into the smoke over the field, not more than fifty feet above it. I was still incredulous because I could see that the planes were bombing the field itself, and things were burning, and I couldn't believe it was nothing more than practice. However, the people who had lived there, which included everyone but Lois Eubank, another graduate student, and me, said it must be practice. I am sure everyone must have considered the possibility that it was a real attack, for we spoke about it and asked one another what it would be like if it were Japan attacking. How innocent we were."

Three of Dr. St. John's four children, two sons and one daughter, were on the hike. Mary, then ten years old, said that when they saw things exploding, the adults were totally convinced that the Army was holding maneuvers because the newspapers had carried stories alerting civilians that war games would be played on the island. They assumed the first big explosion they saw was "some noodlehead dropping a bomb on the Standard Oil of California tanks by mistake."

Conger was fascinated. "Several planes flew right above us, and I remember looking at them and noticing that they were U.S. planes, for I could see the markings on their rudders, of the type they were using in 1935 or thereabouts and were then using for training pilots after they had graduated from primary training. One group of three pursuit planes flew over, but they were going too fast and I wouldn't have thought of looking at their markings anyway.

"By this time the planes had ceased diving and dropping their bombs on Wheeler Field and were scurrying around practicing ground strafing, so we thought, so we got back in our cars and drove about half a mile further through the fields toward the mountains."

Then the group almost became one of the friendly-fire statistics as American shells began falling to earth near them.

"As we were driving, we noticed that the shells were beginning to drop on the field where we were, which did scare us exceedingly, at least it did me. We stopped, got out to look around, and were scared as more and more shells were dropping in the field. It was then we noticed that the maneuvers had moved down to Pearl Harbor, which was about eight miles from us. We could see planes there, as small specks, and could see the bomb explosions on Ford Island and all around Pearl Harbor.

"And still we thought it was practice. The battleships and other boats in Pearl Harbor were firing like mad; there were hundreds of antiaircraft bursts over the harbor, but it was too far away for us to see if any of the planes were hit. We could see smoke coming up from Ford Island and very plainly could see flashes from guns on the ships.

"About this time more shells began plopping into the field around us. Two landed within a hundred yards of us and exploded, although no shrapnel hit us. The terrifying thing was that we could hear the shells coming, and didn't know when one would hit us. There would be a high, wobbly whistle in the air, which would gradually go down in pitch as the shell came nearer, and soon it would land and explode. I frankly admit that my heart was in my mouth and I was scared to death. Actually, I don't believe more than ten shells landed near us, but that was enough.

"As soon as the shells stopped coming, everyone got very indignant about the whole thing and Mrs. Richardson, who was secretary to an admiral or something at Pearl Harbor, said she was going to give him hell the next morning for firing the guns up in the mountains without any announcement in the paper or radio.

"We again turned toward Pearl Harbor, and every time I saw one of the guns fire, I quaked in my boots while waiting for the scream of a shell, but no more came our way. Smoke was coming up from Ford Island, which obscured much of the harbor, but we could still see the ships firing and shells bursting in the air. Wheeler Field was hidden behind a great cloud of smoke and seemed to have quieted down.

"Shortly after the shells stopped landing, we drove the rest of the way to the edge of the field and began our hike up into the mountains. It was the first time I had been in the Wainais, and the vegetation is quite different from the Koolau Range. It was a hard hike going up, during which we went up about 1,500 feet, and got to the top at 2,700 feet. At odd intervals on the way up we would hear the guns firing again, and we would listen for the shells, but none came.

"We spent the whole day there, collecting plants and looking at things new to us. From the peak we could see all over the island. Wheeler and Pearl Harbor were still burning, and it was then that I became certain something had happened to Pearl Harbor because the smoke coming from it was a dense black, and I was sure it was oil smoke, though I still thought it was an accident.

"The trip down was uneventful. I was worn out when we got back to the cars at about 5:30. The sun was beginning to go down by the time we started home.

"It got dark before we reached Pearl Harbor and we turned on our lights, although everybody else was driving with blue lights, if they had any on at all. Army trucks were tearing by in both directions, passing us on both sides, which made Mrs. Richardson quite angry; we had a five-minute tirade on the recklessness of the Army truck drivers, all the accidents they were responsible for, etc.

"When we came to the rotary where our road joined the Pearl Harbor road, five or six military police were standing there, but none said anything about our lights. We drove on until we reached Red Hill, near Pearl Harbor but above it, and stopped to look at the blaze on Ford Island about a mile away. It was on the same dock I had worked on when I first came to Hawaii in September.

"A mile further on, several Boy Scouts stopped us and ordered us to turn out our lights. When we asked why, they said simply, 'Japan has attacked us,' and in a flash the whole thing became clear to us. All the planes, all the bombing, all the shooting, all the fires we had seen that morning had been due to the Japanese.

"After we turned out our car lights, it was so dark that Dr. Richardson couldn't see to drive, so I got out and dogtrotted along the curb for the last mile so that he could follow my white shirt and stay on the road. It was rather frightening getting there. All the houses were dark and no lights on the street, until suddenly a military policeman would flash a light and stop us, inspect us and let us go. It seemed as though it must be four in the morning, but when I realized it was only about 7:30 in the evening, it made me think I was in a city of the dead.

"The first people we talked to were neighbors of the Richardsons, who came over as soon as we arrived. They told us that the Japs had demol-

ished every airfield on the island: Wheeler, Hickam, Kaneohe, Pearl Harbor, Belling, and that hardly a plane had been able to get off the ground. All the ships had been trapped in Pearl Harbor and had tried to get out into the sea.

"After more exchange of news, we went into the Richardsons' house, stumbled around in the dark, tried to hang rugs, curtains, and blankets over the windows, but were unable to black out anything but the kitchen. Mrs. Richardson made some soup for us, the only thing she could prepare. I had Campbell's onion soup, a trivial detail but I had only a small can of cold baked beans and was hungry as a bear, and a glass of port. The food made us all feel better.

"I called Louisa Palmer, a friend of my mother who was teaching at the university, because she was the only person in Hawaii who might have wondered about me.

"Lois and I left at about 8:30, and Mrs. Richardson said that she imagined we would never forget each other after the experience of spending the first day of the war together. I thought she was right.

"Lois and I walked about two miles home. It was dark and raining by this time, and occasionally a star would peek through a hole in the clouds. The streets were practically deserted, the only indication of life being an occasional flash of light from a soldier on guard on a street corner.

"I felt extremely depressed and down in the dumps. I didn't feel any resentment or anger against anyone. The whole affair made me so sad I could have wept. It is impossible that the world population wants anything like this. As we walked up Manoa Road, which goes up Punahou Hill behind Punahou School, I was impressed with the darkness of the city spread out below, from Diamond Head to Pearl Harbor.

"We got to Lois's without incident, and her sister was in when we arrived, her ear glued to her radio. From there I went to see Louisa, and she had sent some cablegrams that morning. I asked her to send one home for me saying, 'Safe. Tell Pris.' Pris was Priscilla Nash, who four years later became my wife.

"Then I toddled home through the dark and was stopped by some American Legionnaires on duty at the corner of Oahu and Kamehameha, chatted with them for a minute and went on home."

The St. John family had an equally exciting evening.

"My father was always the last to leave because he wanted to be sure everyone was accounted for when we left the mountains," Mary St. John Zemach said. "By the time we left, it was getting dark and we had the car lights on.

"My brother Charles had just got his driver's license and was driving, and we started off down the highway, which at that time had three lanes, two regular lanes and a center lane for passing. We hadn't gone far until a motorcycle came up behind us and the man shouted, 'Watch your lights, buddy!' We didn't know what the problem was. Someone thought perhaps he meant Charles should turn the beam up, so he did.

"Shortly after that we were stopped by a policeman. He looked inside the car and said, 'My God, it's Dr. St. John.' He was a former botany student, and he knew instantly what we were doing and why we hadn't heard anything. He told us we were at war and said he was supposed to make all civilians spend the night beside the road, but since he knew my father, he had us follow him to the Pearl City police station to have our lights painted over.

"My father took over the driving and drove down the middle lane with no lights on, and it was one of the scariest rides I've ever been on. We got to Pearl City alive and someone painted out our lights with a rolled-up newspaper dipped in dark blue ink. . . .

"Then they told us we could try to get to Honolulu but there was no guarantee we could make it. The policeman warned us to use the lights as little as possible because some civilians were shooting at headlights. So we took off again. There was no moon but just enough light from the stars to see a little. To make it worse for us, most streets in those days were covered by large trees. . . . So it was really difficult.

"Every time we blinked on the lights to see where we were, people shouted at us, and we assumed they were trigger-happy people.

"We got home and rolled into the driveway and my mother rushed out, peered into the car to count heads, and without saying anything else, said, 'Harold, there's a Navy wife in the basement with a loaded revolver. Would you please take it away from her?'

"She and my little sister, who was eight, had stayed home because it was a long hike, too long for my sister, who wasn't a strong hiker yet. They had started to walk to church—we didn't have a radio because my father disapproved of them—so she didn't know what had happened. They hadn't gone very far before an elderly woman rushed out onto her porch and said, 'Mrs. St. John, you must get off the street immediately!'

"My mother thought, 'Oh dear, Mrs. ——— has finally gone over the edge.'

" 'It's all right,' mother told her. 'We're just going to church.'

"The woman was insistent, so my mother and sister went into the

house to calm the lady, and then they heard the news. They turned around and walked home.

"My mother was a very unflappable sort of person, so she decided that things would be getting more lively than less as the day went on, so while things were still quiet, decided she had better do Monday's laundry. So they gathered up everything that was dirty and did the washing. She filled the bathtub and filled bottles with water. She was hanging out the last of the clothes when the doorbell rang. It was a military officer, who handed her a sheaf of papers and said, 'Your husband is in charge of this block and here are his orders.'

"She had already calculated that we were all past Pearl Harbor when the attack came, but thought we might have trouble getting home, so she told the officer her husband was out of town and explained the circumstances. He said he didn't have time to appoint anyone else and she was in charge. So she took her orders, which were (1) show everyone on the block where to shut off their water and gas, and (2) keep everyone calm.

"There were no men left in the neighborhood at all. The military men had all reported back to their posts, and all the able-bodied men had been called out either to dig graves or donate blood. So only women and children were left at home, and most women didn't know where to turn off the water and gas. It took my mother the rest of the afternoon to go around the block getting all of this done. She found that most people were a lot less interested in how to turn off their water and gas than the question that was on everyone's mind: what to do when the Japanese came back, because everyone was convinced they would return for the invasion.

"In the middle of our block was a small hill with two houses on it, both of which had basements beneath them. Ours was one of them, so she divided the block in half and assigned everyone to one of these two houses. I believe we had twenty-one or twenty-two people in our basement, and by the time we got home, my mother had blacked out the basement and had given everyone dinner. My sister and I went downstairs to sleep with the others, but it was too noisy and we went back upstairs. People slept there several nights, but each night there were fewer. The last to go slept there about a week."

Dr. St. John was not the only University of Hawaii professor who did not know of the attack.

"A professor and his wife were moving that weekend," Mary St. John

Zemach said, "and they were too busy to turn on a radio while they hauled things back and forth. They finally finished on Sunday night and sat down to have dinner and turned on the lights.

"It wasn't long before a neighbor came over and asked what they thought they were doing with their lights on. 'Can't you see that everyone in Honolulu has their lights out?' The professor looked out across the city and, sure enough, not a light was showing anywhere. They didn't know what it was all about but felt silly asking the neighbor, so they turned off the lights and went to bed.

"The next morning he got into his car and drove down to the campus, and when he got to the university he was stopped by an armed sentry.

" 'Halt! What do you think you're doing?' the sentry asked.

" 'What do you think *you're* doing?' the professor retorted. 'I'm going to teach my classes.'

"Then the sentry told him what had happened, so he turned around and drove home to tell his wife."

6

Friendly Fire

Among the civilians deeply involved in the attack were members of the Honolulu Fire Department, the only civilian fire department in America that has fought fires caused by war. Three civilian firemen were killed that day and five others were wounded. A sixth was wounded two days later when a bomb exploded.

The shells landed all over Honolulu, from out on Diamond Head to the foothills of the mountains to the Pali Highway. More fell on downtown Honolulu than elsewhere, including a cluster that hit on McCully near South King Street, setting fires that leveled a block of stores and homes, and put thirty-one families out of homes.

At the time, everyone assumed that the fires were caused by incendiary bombs, but later the firefighters and military leaders determined that the explosions were from American shells, and the accompanying fires were usually caused by wind- or fire-blown sparks hitting the tinder-dry frame buildings which characterized Honolulu at that time. There was an occasional exception, of course, such as a house fire near Aiea and one in a cane field, both of which were caused by Japanese planes crashing. All told, the property damage was estimated at $500,000, a considerable sum at that time.

About three dozen explosions were pinpointed on city maps, of which four or five caused major fires. In addition to the McCully and South King Street fires, explosions occurred in Pacific Heights, on Fort and School streets, at the News Building on Kapiolani, and at the Lewers and Cooke Building in downtown Honolulu.

Among the sixty-eight civilians killed was a group of amateur boxers standing at a food stand that sold the Oriental dish called *saimin* on the corner of Nuuanu and Kukui streets. A woman in the Nuuanu Valley was killed, and four shipyard workers were rushing to Pearl Harbor when their car was hit on Judd Street. Another man was killed by shrapnel while standing across the street from the governor's mansion when a shell hit the mansion grounds.

The firemen's first thought when they heard the news or saw planes flying overhead with the Rising Sun painted on the fuselage was to head for the firehouse, whether they were on duty or not. Some were in church when they heard the explosions, and one was helping a neighbor repair a fence. Although the day was confusing for the firemen—they had been trained to fight fire, not war—those who did not report to the target areas responded to thirty-nine alarms that day. Nearly all of these were caused by American shells hitting homes and buildings.

Richard L. Young, who retired as department chief, was then a rookie fireman and always remembered the ride out to Hickam from the station in Kalihi on the back of a hose wagon. They roared out past Moanalua Gardens, down Puuloa Road, and over Kamehameha Highway, passing stopped cars with people looking up at the planes. When they entered Hickam's main gate, they saw the destruction and dead bodies everywhere.

They arrived just as the second wave of Japanese planes came in; that was when the three firemen were killed and several others wounded.

When the last attack ended, the firemen went to work, first trying to save lives until the military apparatus went into high gear and the civilian volunteers began streaming in to help.

The firemen in the target area fought fires all through the day and the night. Many of the fire mains had been severed by bombs, so the firemen sucked water from the craters.

One off-duty hoseman, Alexander K. Beck, called in as soon as he heard of the attack and was told his fire engine had already left for Hickam Field, but that he was needed at another station in Kakaako. He picked up the engine there, found two volunteers, roared back to his regular station at Palama, loaded on some hose, and went to war.

"We responded to a call to go to a gas tank fire in Iwilei," he said. "A shell had blasted a hole through the top of the tank, which was nearly full, and gas was shooting up through the hole and making a spectacular flame."

It took two hours to contain it. The firemen and volunteers were joined by gas-company men and other volunteers as they built a dike of sandbags around the hole, then began pouring water and foam in.

Beck went back to the station and saw some of the engines coming in from Hickam and heard of the casualties—deaths and injuries—his friends had suffered. Some engines were badly damaged by machine-gun fire and shrapnel. One engine had been hit in the radiator, and Beck repaired it with brown soap and toilet paper he bought at a little store next door to the fire station.

In 1944 the firemen who were killed or injured were awarded Purple Hearts by the Army, an unusual honor for civilians.

Robert Wenkham was still new to Hawaii. He was working on his first job, as a civil engineer for the Army Corps of Engineers. He had arrived on September 16, 1941, after being hired on the mainland by a recruiter who gave him a one-way, first-class ticket on the Matson Line's *Lurline*.

A lifelong environmentalist, Wenkham was up early that Sunday morning to go hiking with the Hawaiian Trail and Mountain Club along a ridge above Mokulei'a from Makua to Ka'ena Point.

"We gathered at our regular meeting place, the downtown Army-Navy YMCA," he said. "We were on our way before eight o'clock, approaching Pearl Harbor, when we noticed several unusual aircraft overhead.

"I recognized the Japanese red 'meatball' insignia at the same time I saw billowing clouds of black smoke over Pearl Harbor. This was obviously no elaborate naval rehearsal, so I changed my schedule for the day to walk the streets of Honolulu and see what happened. I had brought my small folding Kodak Retina with me for pictures on the trail. Perhaps I might photograph the beginning of the war if I could get close enough.

"I left the car behind and walked up into Alewa Heights, a residential area, until I was sufficiently high for an unobstructed view over Pearl Harbor. It was like opening a page of *Life* magazine in full color, three dimensions, and sound. Hearing the rumble of distant explosions, black smoke mixed with splashes of bright orange, and small airplanes darting swiftly about was like watching an old war movie. Silver planes occasionally dived toward the earth and as quickly returned, into a sky peppered with small splotches that suddenly appeared, as if Jackson Pollock was creating a giant landscape by throwing buckets of black paint against the sky. It was frightening to watch."

Soon Wenkham, like many other civilians, almost became a victim of the American military effort. As the shore batteries and ship guns began firing at the planes overhead, the American shells began landing in and around Honolulu. Many of the antiaircraft shells failed to explode in the air but did so on contact with the ground, as did the five-inch cannon shells from the ships.

When the fighting was over and investigations completed, the consensus was that only one bomb from a Japanese plane fell in Honolulu, and it was believed that was an accident. A total of 68 civilians were killed during the attack, about 50 were hospitalized, and 230 slightly injured—most as the result of American shells. While most of the civilian casualties were in Honolulu, two were killed at Waipahu and three in Wahiawa.

Much of the problem was from defective antiaircraft ammunition. It was supposed to explode at a preset altitude, but much of it did not and fell back to the earth, where it exploded on contact, giving the appearance of bombs. A coast artillery officer said he was certain the damage was caused by the five-inch projectiles because he saw them landing, and in fact one shell had hit one of his mortars on Diamond Head.

"As I stood with my mouth agape, asking myself what happens now," Wenkham said, "I heard the sound of a faint whistle, becoming louder and louder as it obviously moved closer. I took it to be the sound of falling bombs whistling in the air as they fell. Puffs of gray smoke rising above nearby homes, followed by muffled explosions, verified that the neighborhood was under attack and that I should find shelter. I looked around me, not knowing quite what to do, then I saw the flash of an explosion in the next block. Quickly I rolled into the nearest gutter, lying as flat as possible, as the whistling grew uncomfortably loud, headed directly toward me. [It] exploded with a sharp bang in the middle of the street a few yards away, shrapnel pieces whistling outward in every direction. I heard them pass within inches of my ears and watched in amazement as the white paint of the wood cottage behind me instantly acquired dozens of black holes, the shrapnel spraying through the house like someone shaking black pepper on a baked potato. I didn't know the exposure, but I took some pictures anyway.

"I waited until I heard no more whistling and stood up, shaking dust and dirt off my hiking clothes. In the street a new 1941 Packard sedan had stopped, its engine still running, a strange hum in the eerie silence. I walked over, curious, noting that the automobile, too, was punctured everywhere with the same black holes. I looked inside. The passengers had red holes, and the man nearest me was trying to hold his arm together, the bone protruding from torn flesh. There was no way I could help them.

"I finished the roll of film and walked back down the hill. Several friends were waiting for me on the front lanai of my apartment on Judd Street and asked what I had seen. I started to tell them, but I could only open my mouth. I could not utter a sound. I was in shock, and it was several hours before I was able to talk coherently about the beginning of the war.

"On Monday I delivered my film to Wadsworth's Camera Shop for processing, and on Tuesday, U.S. Navy Intelligence confiscated my film. When the next issue of *The Saturday Evening Post* magazine arrived in Honolulu, I saw my pictures spread across four pages, with captions telling of the death and destruction by the Japanese bombing of Honolulu. They were not my captions, but they were my first published photographs. Their appearance encouraged me to take photography seriously."

Wenkham forgot about the film as the war wore on and he stayed in the islands, specializing in the design of water and sewage systems on several Pacific Islands. He also operated a successful commercial photography business. Not long after the war ended, he received an envelope from the Navy, and inside was his confiscated film.

"Just like that," he said. "No explanation or anything. I still have the film."

7

A Chinese-American Family

Frederick W. Chou, then thirteen, had returned with his family from Shanghai the previous May to their home on Lewalani Drive, across the street from Roosevelt High School. That was before the landmark banyan tree was planted on the school's front lawn, he said, and his aunts used to have great fun sliding down the steep lawn on large ti plant leaves. The house had a view of the entire Waikiki Beach, and the only hotels they could see were the Royal Hawaiian and Ala Moana.

The Pearl Harbor attack affected his life and the lives of other Orientals in Hawaii in many ways. Some of the effects were positive because, as Chou points out, the war broke down many of the racial and social barriers.

On the Saturday before the attack, his aunt and uncle and their two children came to spend the night with Frederick's family, so he and his father shared the sofa in the living room.

"Around seven in the morning we heard a noise in the sky. It was like airplanes doing some stunts or practicing. I thought nothing of it, since the Army did this sort of thing frequently. However, my aunt, who loved to sleep late on Sundays, looked out the window and exclaimed, 'Why do they have to practice so early?'

"My father, who was just returning to private medical practice, said, 'Never mind, I have an appointment this morning.' So he got dressed and asked me if I would like to accompany him on his walk to the office. The distance was about two miles. Ordinarily we would have taken the tram car. In Honolulu they had just gotten rid of streetcars and were using trams. However, the fare was a nickel, and as we had just returned from China, where my father was earning Chinese dollars (yuan), we felt the poverty, since the exchange rate to U.S. dollars was 20 to 1 at that time. Spending a nickel seemed like spending a Chinese dollar.

"As we walked up the hill toward Punchbowl Crater, we noticed a barrage of gunfire from Punchbowl, and we kept wondering what kind of special practice was going on. Some of the smoke was white, some was dark. As we walked over the rise at the foot of Punchbowl, we saw great billows of smoke coming from around the ships at Pearl Harbor. There seemed to be some flames around the ships, but then, as we could not see very clearly, we just thought that it was more of the Navy's practice. My father suggested that the Navy was putting up some kind of smoke screen.

" 'Only Uncle Sam has that kind of money to burn,' he said."

Looking back on it, Chou sees the day as symbolic of the end of white supremacy in Hawaii, and to him the Pacific Club represented that supremacy. The club was across the street from his father's office, so he was very aware of it.

"There stood the Pacific Club, set back from the street, its long driveway through lava rock entrances flanked on both sides by great monkeypod trees. This was the great bastion of oligarchic power of the Big Five of the islands. [The Big Five were the five major family-owned businesses that controlled most of Hawaiian commerce: sugar, pineapples, docks, shipping, and merchandising. The families who composed the Big Five included the Doles, Thurstons, Alexanders, Baldwins, Castles, and Cookes. They gained even more power by intermarrying. Their companies, which still exist, are C. Brewer & Co., Theo. H. Davies & Co., Amfac (American Factors), Castle & Cooke, and Alexander & Baldwin.]

"Here lay the center of *haole* [white] supremacy in Hawaii for decades," Chou continued. "Here was the cumulative oligarchic power of the sugar interests for the plantation life, for the domination over the Asiatics for cheap labor, and hence for money and power. Little did anyone suspect that the events of this day would overturn the power of the white elite and render it into the hands of those they suppressed for decades.

"My father's office was a small, white single-story house that had belonged to my grandmother. My father had evicted the tenants and refurbished it as an office again, and when I was a boy of five, I used to watch the streetcars come up and down Emma Street, which was at the end of the line, and they would pull down the contacts from the overhanging electric wires and swing them around to return to downtown Honolulu.

"We got to the office a few minutes before eight. The air was already quite warm and the office was stuffy. My father opened the doors and windows to air out the place, and then we sat on the front stoop to watch the people walk by. Everyone seemed to be rushing up Punchbowl Hill with bags and possessions. They were mostly Japanese, and we thought they were silly trying to carry their belongings up the side of Punchbowl, and we wondered if indeed something was going on that we did not know about.

"The sounds of gunfire were quite loud at times, and we wondered where they were shooting from. One particular blast shook the whole office. My father began to get bored and asked me to go to the corner store to buy the . . . *Star Bulletin.* I went down and asked but was told that all the papers were sold.

"Still bored and curious, my father then asked me to run down to get the . . . *Advertiser.* I ran down again, but the Chinese man said, 'No come yet.' [The *Advertiser* was late due to a power outage that delayed the printing, causing some people to mistakenly assume Japanese spies had sabotaged the printing press.] My father, in disgust, turned on the old Zenith radio that we had in the office. It had the shape of an upside-down parabola with two small knobs and a small dial with a small speaker. The newscaster was saying, 'This is an air-raid attack! Get off the streets!' My father turned the radio off. 'What would they do if the real thing happened?' he grunted.

"It was about 8:30 now, and we could hear police whistles blowing and the ambulance and firehouse sirens sounding. We stood on the sidewalk and looked down the street and saw nothing but ambulances going back and forth from Queens Hospital, which was only two blocks from the office, wondering what they were doing. We were unaware that shortly some of those kids running down the street would be United States soldiers, fighting in the 442nd Infantry Division, and would earn the right to a GI Bill, a free education, and eventual political power. They would someday overthrow those who were now represented by the great symbol, the Pacific Club.

"The noise and excitement were too much for my father. He decided to investigate, rationalizing that his patient wasn't coming anyway, so we closed the office, locked the windows and the front door, and walked down Emma Street.

"We met the Chinese minister of the Chinese Congregational Church, and he was holding a piece of shrapnel that he said the Japanese were using to bomb us. . . . The vernier tip had the words Ford Motor Company inscribed with its famous logo, and we were puzzled by it. Later on, I concluded that it was a piece of shell from our own antiaircraft guns.

"A man arrived with a World War I tin hat . . . a clipboard and a gas mask, that ubiquitous piece of equipment we all had to carry around with us for the next three years. He had an arm band with a couple of . . . half triangles printed on it indicating he was from the Civil Defense, and wore leggings in the style of World War I soldiers. And he had an authoritative air about him.

"He told everyone that the radio stations KGU and KGMB would go off the air at noon so that enemy aircraft could not home in on the broadcast, and he said there was to be a total blackout. No light was to escape from the house, and we should fill all our containers with water just in case the enemy should poison or destroy our water supply.

"With that, we all went into the house, had lunch, took baths and filled the tubs with water, and waited for night to come. The radio stations went off the air as scheduled, and in place we listened to the paranoiac police broadcasts. All through the night the radio kept referring to possible parachute landings, lights to be checked out, and so forth. Although there wasn't supposed to be any traffic, cars with headlights covered over with black tape, except for a small hole one inch in diameter that emitted a blue light, were traveling continually.

"My uncles were in despair. They acted like cattle in a pen waiting to be killed. One wanted to give up his printing business to those who worked for him because he was sure he was going to be captured and die at the hands of the Japanese invaders. My father had other thoughts and wondered why the Japanese were so stupid to attack America, unless they really planned a great invasion of America to march toward Washington. He could not understand how the Japanese could bring . . . such folly on themselves.

"I was excited. All the schools were closed, including the Catholic school, Maryknoll, that I was attending. No more catechism; no more Christmas pageant for me. I had been scheduled to act in a Christmas pageant as one of the shepherds standing half naked with a leopard skin and crooked staff in one hand. The thought of doing that was far more distressing than the bombs dropping. Furthermore, I had already experienced Japanese bombs dropping in the vicinity of Shanghai, and the prospect of more bombs didn't bother me. As for changes in schools, I had already gone to some thirty different schools in Shanghai in 1937 and 1938.

"All of us stayed up to wait and listen to the police reports."

8

Hell on a Sunshiny Day

Linore Tiffany moved to Honolulu in 1937 as a dietician and was married in 1939. When the attack occurred, she and her husband were in the kitchen; he was working a crossword puzzle he had found. He was an early riser on Sundays so he could work the crossword puzzle in the *Honolulu Advertiser,* which was late that morning because of a press breakdown.

"I was feeding Paul [our son] while my husband sat in his bathrobe working on the puzzle when we heard the first boom. We looked at each other expectantly because it was only about three blocks from where we lived, and the Navy had decided to blast out some basalt to make a storage tunnel. They usually did the blasting on Sunday, and they always sent a card to tell us when they were going to to it. But neither of us had seen one.

"The next boom was closer, and my husband got dressed quickly and was starting out the door when a little fat sergeant came running down the street with a megaphone, telling all the women and children to go to the cold storage tank. We weren't supposed to know the storage tank existed, for security reasons, but of course we all did.

"I had to walk down a block and a half from the house, then start up an incline to get to the tunnel. There were about 100 of us, and half of the women and children had been to church and were all dressed up. The other half were in nightgowns and muumuus and robes. We were a motley crew. I had grabbed Paul, my coat, a package of cigarettes, and a lipstick, and that was all. No diapers, no food, nothing. As we went into the tunnel, the Navy began hauling out sticks of dynamite they had stored in there.

"Nobody knew where their husbands were, if they were dead or alive, and of course there were no toilet facilities. They finally decided to do something for us and brought in cots, and said only pregnant women could use them. I was pregnant, so I got a cot. The next problem was water; we were afraid to drink it because it might be poisoned.

"Then the Army gave us latrines; they dug a hole and put a ladder over the hole, and strung wire around and put up Army blankets for privacy. But the blankets wouldn't fit to the top of the hole, so when you sat there, everyone had a clear view. One pregnant woman got stuck in the ladder, and of course there was no way to wash later. . . .

"During all of this, one woman had a nail file and she just kept filing her nails, hour after hour.

"I had a fabulous neighbor who was born and reared in Honolulu, and her baby was two weeks younger than mine. I had shouted at her when we were being evacuated to hurry. She said she'd be there in a few minutes, so I went on ahead. She grabbed a lot of equipment, milk, food, diapers, and put them in a sack.

"We had a giant lightbulb on all the time that kept us from sleeping, and with kids screaming and mothers walking up and down, we couldn't move around much. Finally, that afternoon they told us to go home, but they had put up alarms all over the fort, and if we heard them, we had to go immediately to the tunnel. The klaxon horn in our area was on a garage right across the street from our house.

"After two or three false alarms and grabbing Paul and running, I got wise and decided that was silly and would get under a bed instead. Soldiers were ordered to search houses, but they never found us under the beds. They'd come in the front and shout, 'Anybody here?' and go right out the back door."

When the war began, Edwin A. Weber was manager of the Wahlawa Plantation that belonged to the Hawaiian Pineapple Corporation. He and his family lived in the town of Waiawa, which is in the center of Oahu and adjacent to Schofield Army Barracks and Wheeler Field.

On that Sunday morning he and three friends, L. P. Young, Red Hendrie, and George Kinney, were playing a round of golf on the Kalakaua Golf Course at Schofield. Although none of them were attached to a military unit—all worked for the same company—the Army allowed personnel of some companies to use the course.

The men teed off at 7:30 that morning, and while they were finishing the first hole, they saw a flight of planes coming through Kolekole Pass in the Waianae Range just a few miles away. The planes passed directly overhead, and the next thing they heard was the explosions at Wheeler Field, two miles away.

The men kept playing because they had no idea what was happening. As they were teeing up on the second hole, a confused Army sergeant with a machine gun came running across the course and jumped into the sand trap next to them. The men stood in stunned silence and watched. The sergeant shouted at them to get off the golf course. "Now!"

They asked what on earth was going on, and the sergeant admitted he did not exactly know, but "we are under attack and we've all been issued live ammo." That was enough for the golfers. They ran.

That is not quite all of the story. Exactly eleven years later at 7:55 A.M. the four men met to resume the game that had been so dramatically interrupted. They teed up again on the second hole of Kalakaua Golf Course and finished their game.

Lois Cartwright was a young bride in Honolulu and went with her husband and a Navy chaplain to Pearl Harbor to sing on one of the ships. The attack occurred just before they arrived, and they were turned away at the gate. They were taken over to Hickam Field to catch a bus.

When they returned home, they knocked on the door of a young Navy officer who was what they called a "ninety-day wonder" because he had gone through Officers Candidate School. They told him of the attack and he did not believe them. "Really," he sniffed. "If that had happened, I would have been notified." After thus chastising them, he slammed the door. They do not know where he was sent, but they never saw him again.

Since the attack was so far from the norm, people often reacted accordingly, saying and doing things that later made them question their sanity.

"I knew a woman who was living near Hickam Field who had planned a cocktail party for other officers and wives that afternoon," Lois Malone said. "She told me later that at the height of the attack, she called her guests to say, 'If this keeps up, we'll just have to cancel the party.' She told me she was surely in mild shock to have said that."

Perhaps this is one of those stories which become folklore and cannot be authenticated. It involves a motor launch that several Navy officers had taken at a dock. They headed out to their ship in it. When they reached the ship, one of the officers pulled the wheel over, tied it, and let the boat go, circling around in the chaos.

Lee Barnwell Thomassen, then a young woman in Honolulu, was told the story by one of the officers who was aboard the boat.

"In Charleston, South Carolina, about two years later I was talking to the brother of an uncle by marriage, and he told me that he and several of his men had to abandon their ship. While they were in the water, they saw a motor launch circling and were able to climb aboard it and got to shore. We all believe it was the same boat."

Her father, a radiologist (then called roentgenologist) and head of Tripler General Hospital's X-ray section, went to the hospital as soon as he heard of the attack. He did not return home for three days.

"He told me our own soldiers, young green troops mostly, were more dangerous than the enemy might have been. One of those nights he had lain down on an X-ray table for a nap and a machine gun went off, tracing a line of bullets just inches above his head. No one knew he was there and he was well liked, so he was sure it was an accident.

"About the same time his car received forty-two bullet holes. His men painted wound stripes above them."

As the hours and days wore on and the fear of invasion was as real as the actual attack, Lee learned that "you can't live in a high state of terror very long. The mind simply forbids it. You get used to living with fear and you learn to live around it.

"Also, almost immediately the most extraordinary change took place in the people. I look back on that time almost with nostalgia because we all began talking to each other and trusting one another. No longer did I refuse rides with strangers, for instance. We all felt we were in it together, which indeed we were on this island with no escape."

Marlene Peterson was ten years old when war came. Her father was a deep-sea diver in charge of the escape training tank at Pearl Harbor. On that Sunday morning she and her two younger brothers were just leaving their home in the Navy housing section for church at the Block Arena when the planes came.

"As we went out the door, we saw the planes and heard the explosions, and men were running through the streets trying to get back to the base.

"Bullets were hitting all around, and one hit the front steps right where we were standing. We ran back into the house yelling, and ran upstairs, where another bullet came through the roof and lodged in the hallway floor. My father was yelling at us to go downstairs and get under the table, and then he took off for the base.

"Later in the morning some buses came and we were told to get on them. My mother told me to go in the kitchen and get the bag of fruit she had just bought, but instead I grabbed my cat, and off we went. The bus took us to the YMCA in Honolulu, which was hectic at that point. My mother found a man to drive us to the Sacred Heart Convent, the school we attended, and the nuns took us in and my mother went back to Pearl Harbor to try and help.

"We didn't see her again for several weeks. I later found out that my father was diving on the sunken ships and trying to get some of the guys out. He said he had to go past one of the Japanese subs that was sunk in the harbor . . . the man had tried to get out but only his hand made it, and every time my father swam past, the hand seemed to be waving at him.

"The saddest thing he told us, with tears in his eyes, was hearing the men trapped in ships tapping on the insides of the ship for help, and there was no way to get them out. He said he could never forget it. He was awarded the Bronze Star for his work that day."

The three children were evacuated by ship to the mainland. They spent the war in a Catholic boarding school near their grandparents in the Los Angeles area.

The popular radio program "Hawaii Calls" was on when the attack came, and the announcer, Web Edwards, broke into the music and made his first announcement at 8:04, recalling all military personnel to their posts. He repeated it again at 8:15 and at 8:30. He said nothing about the attack itself until 8:40, when he reported "a sporadic attack" and that "the rising sun has been sighted on the wingtips." Some misinterpreted "sporadic" as meaning "simulated," and people began calling the station. Edwards repeated over and over, "This is *no* drill. Pearl Harbor is under attack."

People still could not believe it, and the phones kept ringing. Then Edwards made the announcement in a different way, one that finally convinced everyone: "This is the real McCoy." The phones went silent.

One who heard Edwards's voice was Ed Sheehan, a shipyard worker who had been in the islands long enough to fall totally in love with them. He was sharing a small house with a machinist named Al Sharkay, and it was Sharkay who woke Sheehan in the middle of the attack. Then they heard Edwards announcing that all Pearl Harbor workers should report immediately for duty.

As they drove out, they were aware of how quiet Honolulu was that early Sunday morning, and neither was totally convinced it was a real attack: Perhaps the American military was putting on an impressive exercise to shake people into believing they could be attacked.

"A whistling sound came from the direction of the submarine base and a plane flew over low, less than a hundred feet above our heads," Sheehan said. "We could see the red suns on its wings and the head of the goggled pilot. The Marines lifted their rifles and fired wildly. The plane's guns clattered briefly, digging up pieces of road and clods of dirt, then bulleted on over Hickam. Oddly, in the moment of quiet that followed, someone laughed.

"I think it was then that I began to believe."

Sheehan was sent to one of the docks, and when he walked through the machine shop, he found many men simply standing at their lathes, transfixed. The shop door opened to a long pier with Ford Island directly across from it, and Sheehan was stunned by what he saw.

"It was like looking into Hell on a sunshiny day," he said. "Each of the great battleships, so strong, clean, and powerful yesterday, was in agony, tortured in an inferno of orange flame and vile smoke. Only the cagelike top sections of the masts on the *West Virginia* and *Tennessee* were visible. The *California* looked half-sunk, listing on one side in snapping fires. The *Arizona* was almost completely hidden. . . . The *Oklahoma* had rolled completely over. With her long bottom showing above water, she looked like an immense floating sausage.

"Close by, at dockside, the cruiser *Helena* had been hit and was listing. The minelayer *Oglala,* moored outboard, was being pulled away by tugs."

The second wave of planes soon came in, and "darted like angry birds at the *Nevada,* hitting her again and again. From a distance she seemed to shiver and shrug, but miraculously kept moving. Moments later racking detonations came from the nearby dry-dock area. Concussions followed, pulsing blasts of warm wind.

"I realized those last hits must have been made on the *Pennsylvania, Cassin,* or *Downes*—perhaps all three.

"Then the destroyer *Shaw* was hit, out on the floating dry dock. The eruption was monstrous, appalling. The ship appeared to disintegrate into a million pieces, a gargantuan fireball. The blast sent scraps of metal twisting and flying in all directions, for thousands of feet, in great slow-motion arcs trailing streamers of smoke. I was probably a quarter of a mile away, yet one of the pieces fell at my feet. I picked it up, a curl of steel ripped clean and shiny, handball-sized. I thought of keeping it as a souvenir; it would have made a conversation piece as a paperweight. Then I threw it away."

Then Sheehan became involved in one of those surrealistic situations that often occur in times of great stress.

"A truck raced up and an elderly man got out and asked me for help. His flatbed was covered with cans, and we worked for about ten minutes unloading and placing them by the roadside. While we labored, there was another explosion in the dry dock. But we kept working, not speaking. Then he drove the truck away and I was alone again. To this day I have no idea what was in those cans or why we unloaded them."

9

The Military Takes Over Hawaii

The radio stations were silenced by noon to prevent the enemy from using radio beams for navigation, then put back on the air for brief, important announcements. Radios were the only source of information for the civilians as well as the military. Frequent announcements came for the military to man their posts, and calls came for civilian volunteers and for blood donors. The military and civilian officials had an emergency plan they put into effect, and it included directions for civilians. These were broadcast at intervals throughout the morning and afternoon.

Civilians were told to stay off the streets, not to use their telephones, to keep calm, and to keep the radio on for further information and news. They were to keep their cars off the streets and to drive on lawns if they had to. They were told to fill water buckets for use in case of fire and to attach garden hoses to faucets. In the event of another air raid, they were to stay under cover to avoid being hurt, as many already had been, by shrapnel from antiaircraft guns.

Perhaps the most important announcement after the attack was that martial law was in effect and that the Army had taken over. This came at 4:25 that afternoon. The final commercial radio broadcast that day was at 8:52 P.M., when employees of retail firms doing business with the Army Engineers were ordered to their jobs immediately.

The island was almost swamped by volunteers, who saved many lives and calmed many frightened people. The Honolulu Chamber of Commerce had recently sponsored a blood bank, but it was totally out of blood after sending seventy-five flasks to Tripler Hospital, forty-five to the Navy, and eighty to the Queen's Hospital. Calls for new donors were broadcast and former donors telephoned. Patients at the Queen's Hospital were among the first donors, and before the morning was out, the blood bank was jammed with donors.

The hospitals began sending recuperating patients home to make room for those injured in the attack. Soon 100 were discharged from Queen's and 105 from Leahi Home. Vehicles of all kinds lined up at the military bases as makeshift ambulances to transport the wounded after a call was issued on the radio. Flatbed trucks from plantations, semis, buses, and a variety of old jalopies were lined up on the sides of the highways leading to Pearl Harbor and Schofield Barracks.

Food was gathered wherever it could be found, and impromptu soup kitchens sprang up outside the military bases and around Honolulu for policemen, firemen, the homeless. When they ran out of coffee, they reused the grounds over and over until fresh coffee could be delivered. Merchants opened their stores and handed out merchandise and tools to whoever asked for them, often without asking for money, vouchers, or even signatures.

Public and private schools, churches, the University of Hawaii buildings, social clubs, and recreation centers became temporary homes for people evacuated from military-target areas.

Before martial law went into effect, Territorial Governor Joseph B. Poindexter went on the radio at about 11:15 to announce that he had created an Office of Civil Defense to oversee protection of the territory. His broadcast was interrupted by a false alarm that the Japanese were back for another attack.

About an hour later General Short, who had recovered sufficiently from the shock of the attack, called on the governor and asked him to proclaim martial law. The governor was understandably reluctant to turn over his powers to the Army and argued against it. General Short was persistent and persuasive. He told the governor of the extensive damage at nearly all the military installations, and said he expected the Japanese to launch a landing by Monday morning.

Governor Poindexter still was not eager to turn over the territorial government to the Army. He put General Short off for an hour so he could call the White House for guidance. Short left the governor's office while Poindexter placed a call to the White House through his switchboard. To his dismay, the operator already had the emergency manual with its censorship rules in front of her, and she refused to make it easy for the governor.

"What are you going to talk about?" she demanded, following the rules. The governor's reply was not recorded, but it must not have been pleasant, because the operator got her supervisor, who said it was permissible for the territorial governor of Hawaii to talk to the president of the United States. But the operator was not through making the governor's day more difficult. She kept breaking in, telling the governor to keep the conversation brief.

Poindexter finally got Roosevelt on the line and gave him a report on the attack, and asked for food and planes. Roosevelt told him both had already been ordered and were on their way. Then Poindexter said that General Short was demanding that martial law be established so the Army could take over. He cited Short's fears of an invasion and sabotage by Japanese living on the island. Roosevelt obviously had many things on his mind and wanted to get on with the military and diplomatic side of the war. So he told the governor that he approved of martial law, asked no questions about it, and ended the conversation.

Short returned in an hour, as agreed, and urged Poindexter to establish martial law because he "knew" landing parties were en route to the islands. He insisted that the morning's attack was only a prelude to an all-out invasion. Poindexter asked how long Short thought martial law would last, and Short said he did not know, but that if the morning's attack was a one-time raid only and not part of an invasion, martial law "could be lifted within a reasonably short time." The governor signed the declaration, saying he had never hated to do anything so much in his life. He was told to read his proclamation of emergency on KGU, and did so at about 11:15. His voice quivered with fatigue. As he was ending the brief address, the Army phoned the station to tell him to get off the air because another attack was expected. His aides hustled him into a car.

Martial law in Hawaii lasted almost three years.

As soon as the governor signed the proclamation, the Army got busy with its first order of business: arresting all residents whom Army and Navy Intelligence, the FBI, and local police considered dangerous. Files had been compiled on those suspected of Japanese leanings, and thirteen squads of police went out while the fires were still burning to round them up and place them in the Immigration Station. By the end of the next day they had 482 in custody: 370 Japanese, 98 Germans, and 14 Italians. Another 100 were placed under surveillance.

The governor was not treated well during the crisis. After being bullied by General Short, and a no-win battle with his switchboard operator, his superior, Secretary of the Interior Harold L. Ickes, never known for his diplomacy, called and offered to send a younger man to Honolulu to give Poindexter a hand. The seventy-two-year-old governor, who had already lost most of his power to the Army, told him a younger man was not needed. Ickes backed off.

The commercial radio silence made one of the day's most unlikely heroes, a police radio dispatcher named Jimmy Wong. When all commercial radio stations were ordered off the air, residents were desperate and scanned the dial. Many found the police band near the end of the dial at 1712 kilocycles.

What they heard that day was the slow, deep, calm voice of Jimmy Wong, who had a gentle, dry wit and was apparently unflappable. Listening to his conversations with other policemen and with ambulance drivers and military officials told the citizens more than any commercial radio station could.

Among the situations Wong had to contend with, in addition to the normal police duties, were getting expectant women to the hospital, sending police cars to pick up blood donors, and sending officers to investigate blackout violations. He also took time to tell the policemen where to find Red Cross canteens: "Any car in Kaimuki, go to the end of Kaimuki car line, as there is a hot pot of soup there to keep you warm."

Two of the more intriguing reports concerned what someone thought were signal lights for the Japanese. One was reflections of moonbeams on darkened windows. The other involved a barking dog. A frightened woman called the police to say it was barking in Morse code and she was afraid it was signaling Japanese paratroopers who might already be on the island.

That night Wong had to report a false alarm: "Pearl Harbor is being bombed again," he announced, but it actually was the planes from the *Enterprise* that had been out searching for the Japanese fleet. Now their pilots were coming home, tired, angry, and frustrated, only to be shot at by their own guns. Four of the planes were shot down, but the other two managed to land safely. One did so by coming in with all landing lights on to buzz the field, hoping he would blind the gunners, then circled and came in with no lights. One of the damaged planes crashed into a residential hotel on the Pearl Harbor Peninsula, killing the pilot and destroying the hotel.

"There wasn't a single commercial to destroy the continuity of this most dramatic of radio performances," the *Honolulu Advertiser* wrote of Wong after his death. "As soon as the police department realized the extent to which the citizenry was listening in on their broadcasts, they augmented an additional public service: They began making periodical news reports."

Among the organizations that were called for help that morning was the American Legion, because its members had military experience. In an hour at least three hundred veterans of the Spanish-American War and World War I were in their clubhouses, ready for active duty.

One member remembered the day with a great deal of humor. He said he got out his Winchester rifle with thirty rounds of ammunition, but it had been so long since he had used it, he had forgotten how to load it. Once he figured that out, he started downtown to help quell the street rioting and the paratrooper invasion he was certain had occurred.

Then he realized that with his rifle he might be mistaken for a looter or rioter, so he trudged back home to put on his old uniform, reasoning that it would also help if he had to appear before civilians as an authority figure.

He could not find parts of the uniform and did not remember where he had put them, so he "got mad and bawled out members of the household," for which he was "told to go out and fight the Germans[*sic*] instead of the women folks at home.

"The dog spied my Sam Browne belt on the lanai and dragged it over into the guava bushes in the next lot to chew it at leisure. Recovered it and spanked the dog."

Finally he escaped the hazards of home-front duty and went to join his fellow Legionnaires at the clubhouse, in the safety of the war zone.

The other six Hawaiian islands were much more remote at that time, and it took several days to get mail between the islands. The curtailed radio broadcasts meant they were really cut off from the heat of the battle and the events of the coming days. The islanders were asked to watch for enemy planes and submarines, a request that was taken very seriously, particularly on Hawaii, where the district Civil Defense commander found guards at every crossroad and bridge between Kohala and Hilo, armed with clubs, cane knives, and firearms, "some of which might well have been torn from museum walls." The island took the war more seriously than the others, banning taxis and most private cars from the roads for several days. And, perhaps out of fear of sabotage and uncertainty if their Japanese-American neighbors were spies, strict rules regarding public gatherings were instituted.

10

Niihau Fights Back

One of the most famous incidents of the invasion occurred far to the west on the remote, privately owned island of Niihau. The island is seventy-two square miles and seventeen miles off the coast of Kauai, far to the northwest of Oahu. It has been privately owned since the white men took over the islands and has always been off limits to all but its two hundred or so residents, most of whom are Hawaiian and possess the purest strain of Hawaiian blood remaining in the islands. They are the only people left in the state who speak Hawaiian all the time, with English as a second language. Niihau has never had electricity, telephones, television, firearms, a doctor, liquor, or a jail.

While they certainly are not enslaved by the owners and are free to leave any time they want to, those who live there have chosen to stay in isolation over the generations and to work on the Robinson family plantation and provide its necessary support services. At this writing, the only outsiders who may visit the island without an invitation from the owners are state officials, such as social services and public safety bureaucrats. The island children go to high school on Kauai, then go away to college if they want to. As is often the case with people who grow up in the isolation and protection of an island, Niihau's pull is strong, and most return.

This enforced isolation and ban on casual visitors gnaws at some people, particularly journalists, who like to hint at dark deeds being done by the owners to the Niihauans. There is hardly a guidebook to Hawaii without a complaint about the way the owners protect their private property. Hawaiians know many of these same journalists would complain bitterly that the owners were ruining the island and the last vestiges of pure Hawaiian culture if they opened the island to guests. And since 1989 tourists have been permitted to take helicopter rides over the island with a stop on a remote beach, leading some to believe the palm curtain may be lifting.

In 1941 the residents knew of the strained relations between the United States and Japan, but were not concerned about it. About the only impact the international tension had on the island was when the Army asked the owners to plow furrows across several thousand acres where airplanes might land. The owners complied without complaint.

What no American knew until long after the war ended was that Niihau had figured in the Japanese attack plans. Because it was reasonably close to Oahu and sparsely populated, Commander Mitsuo Fuchida selected Niihau as a rescue point for pilots whose planes were damaged or who were in danger of running out of fuel. He had read in an encyclopedia that it had no American residents, and it seemed to have an adequate place to land a plane. Once there, he reasoned, the pilots could wait in safety to be picked up by a submarine.

On December 7, 1941, while most of the islanders were going to church, they saw two planes flying over, one with a sputtering and smoking engine. They recognized the Japanese insignia, and although they had no way of knowing about the Pearl Harbor attack, they knew something was not right. Soon one of the planes reappeared, a damaged Japanese Zero fighter that made a crash landing in a rocky field. The landing gear caught in a fence, which knocked it off, and the plane skidded in on its belly. A farmer living nearby, Hawila Kaleohano, saw the plane land, and though he was not educated on world events, he was well enough informed to know it was not an American plane.

He went over to the Zero and found the pilot, who was unhurt, struggling with his seat belt. Kaleohano plucked him out of the cockpit, took away his pistol, and grabbed the papers and map the pilot was trying to take out of his shirt. Unable to converse with his prisoner, Kaleohano sent for the only people of Japanese ancestry on the island: Yoshio Harada, a thirty-year-old American citizen who was the Robinsons' caretaker and assistant beekeeper, and Ishimatsu Shintani, an elderly man who had worked on the island for many years.

The pilot was Petty Officer Shigenori Saikaijo. He had been in the first wave of attackers, and his group had attacked Wheeler Field. His Zero was badly damaged by ground fire, and he had staggered northwest to the rendezvous island, as instructed, while a friend flew on to the waiting carriers. Saikaijo finally admitted to the Niihauans that he was in the attack on Pearl Harbor that morning, and the Hawaiians put him under the equivalent of house arrest—after all, where could he go on the small island?—while they waited for the sampan that the owner, Aylmer Robinson, came over in every Monday morning from Kauai.

However, Robinson did not appear because the islands were under martial law and no boats were permitted to leave any of the islands. The Niihauans waited all week, and when the sampan had not arrived by Friday night, they lit a big bonfire on the beach, the signal everyone on Kauai knew meant trouble.

By that afternoon Saikaijo had won Shintani over to his side and had given him about $200 to bribe Kaleohano to burn the military papers. Kaleohano refused to hand them over and told Shintani he had better stay away from the pilot or he would get into serious trouble. Shintani replied that the pilot would kill him if he did not do as he was ordered. He went into hiding until the episode was over.

Saikaijo had been busy while Shintani and Kaleohano talked. A persuasive man, he had talked Harada into getting some firearms. Then the two went on a crime spree. They first went to Kaleohano's house to get the pilot's papers, but could not find them. They next went to the only village on the island, Puuwai, where they set up two machine guns from the wrecked plane and threatened to kill everyone on the island unless Kaleohano was brought to them. They captured Kaahakila Kalimahuluhulu, tied his hands behind him, and told him to go to Harada's wife with a message. He went in the right direction until he was out of sight, then went back and got a friend, Benehakaka Kanahele, to sneak up on the two terrorists and steal their ammunition.

In the meantime, most of the Niihauan women and children had gone into hiding on beaches, in caves, and in the woods while the men watched the two Japanese, waiting for an opportunity to subdue them.

When Kalimahuluhulu did not return, Saikaijo captured Kalimahuluhulu's wife and sent her to look for her husband; as soon as she was out of sight, she ran into the forest. Then Saikaijo and Harada broke into the home of an elderly woman and threatened to kill her is she did not tell them where Kaleohano was. She told them that only God had the power over life and death, and went back to reading her Bible as though they were not there.

By 4 A.M., totally frustrated, they burned Kaleohano's house to the ground, then burned the plane. After dawn they captured Kalimahuluhulu's friend Kanahele and his wife, then sent Kanahele off to look for Kaleohano while holding his wife hostage. He left and stayed out of sight for awhile, then returned, saying he could not find Kaleohano.

Saikaijo threatened to kill the couple as an example. Since he spoke neither English nor Hawaiian, Kanahele appealed to Harada to take the gun away. Harada told Kanahele Saikaijo would kill him if he tried. Then Kanahele took matters into his own hands. When Saikaijo's back was turned, he jumped him. The pilot managed to get his gun hand free, but Kanahele's wife grabbed his hand. Saikaijo shook her off, then shot Kanahele three times at point-blank range, in the stomach, groin, and leg.

When describing the incident later, Kanahele, a very large and powerful man, said that when he was shot, "Then I got mad." He grabbed Saikaijo by a leg and his neck and bashed his head against a stone wall, killing him instantly. Mrs. Kanahele was angry, too, and she attacked Harada, who managed to get away from her long enough to shoot himself in the head. He died a few hours later.

While this was happening, Kaleohano and four other men had taken off at about midnight in a rowboat across the seventeen-mile channel to get help in Kauai. After a sixteen-hour crossing they found Robinson, who enlisted the Army's help and went to his island aboard a lighthouse tender with a lieutenant, thirteen enlisted men, and three civilians. They landed early on Sunday morning and walked the fourteen miles to Puuwai. They confiscated the papers that had worried the pilot so much, and took Kanahele to the hospital at Waimea.

Neither Shintani nor Mrs. Harada was charged. Shintani was interned during the war, and when it ended, he returned to Niihau with his Hawaiian wife. Mrs. Harada moved to Kauai.

Kanahele and Kaleohano were treated as heroes by the Army and the American Legion. The Army took Kanahele to Fort Shafter to receive the Purple Heart and the Medal for Merit, and in 1946 he was awarded the Medal of Freedom. The American Legion gave both men a medal.

11

The Saga of the *Pacific Clipper*

Pan American had been operating its flying boats in the Pacific since its legendary pilot Ed Musick had flown the first Sikorsky clipper from San Francisco to Honolulu on April 16, 1935. Although the route had never been flown by a passenger-carrying plane, Pan American was so confident it would be profitable that crews were building runways, towers, and hotels on Midway and Wake islands before Musick made the pioneering flight.

Now, six years later, the flights were almost commonplace, and four of Pan American's clippers were operating in the Pacific on the morning of December 7. The *Anzac Clipper* was on its way from San Francisco to Honolulu. The *Philippine Clipper* was sitting in the lagoon at Wake Island, ready to resume its flight to the Orient; the *Hong Kong Clipper* was in Hong Kong Harbor; and the *Pacific Clipper* was in the air between New Caledonia and New Zealand.

Each plane was equipped with an envelope of sealed orders telling the captain what to do in case war did break out. The basic instructions were the same for each crew: Their first responsibility was the safety of passengers and evacuation of all ground personnel possible; they were to maintain radio silence and to alter their course; to fly with no exterior lights and with windows covered; to guard or destroy all mail being carried. In addition, each plane had specific instructions relating to the route it flew. That morning every plane captain flying anywhere in the world tore open the envelope.

Captain H. Lanier Turner's *Anzac Clipper* was still about an hour east of Honolulu when he received a message that war had broken out. He tore open his envelope; his orders told him to divert to Hilo, about 150 miles from Honolulu, on the island of Hawaii. Without telling the passengers, who were just starting their breakfasts, Turner gently banked the big plane and angled south to the village of Hilo.

He told the passengers nothing until after they had landed. Then he called them into the plane's lounge and explained the situation. He gave them a choice of staying in Hawaii on their own or returning to San Francisco with the plane and crew that day. All the passengers chose to remain, so the crew of eleven deadheaded back to San Francisco without incident.

The *Philippine Clipper* had a less easy time. Captain John Hamilton had taken off from the Wake Island lagoon en route to Guam and Manila, where his passengers would be met by the *Hong Kong Clipper* and taken on to Hong Kong. Hamilton was about half an hour into the flight when news of the attack came. He quickly opened his sealed orders, which told him his primary job was to evacuate Pan American employees from Wake Island. So he turned around, dumped more than a ton of gasoline, and landed in the Wake lagoon.

Hamilton talked to the Navy and Marine officers, who had as protection twelve Grumman Wildcats the *Enterprise* had delivered a day or two earlier. But the planes had no reliable navigation system; they were designed to fight only within visual range of Wake. The military commanders asked Hamilton to lead a squadron of fighters on patrol in search of the Japanese fleet they assumed would be coming in that morning. Hamilton made a deal with them: He would lead the patrol in exchange for enough fuel to get him back to Midway, plus enough for the four-hour patrol.

They agreed and refueled the *Philippine Clipper*. She was sitting on the lagoon when eighteen Japanese planes attacked. They strafed and bombed everything on both the Pan American side of the island and the military side. Fuel storage tanks exploded, and buildings and docks disappeared. The Japanese made two passes, leaving severe damage behind them.

But the *Philippine Clipper* still sat at the dock, big and safe. Hamilton ran to the plane and checked her over. Although she was riddled with bullet holes, none of the fuel tanks or engines had been hit. He loaded the plane with his passengers and all the Pan American employees except one who chose to stay and fight, a total of sixty people, two of whom were wounded. The plane was badly overloaded, and Hamilton did not know if he could get her out of the water.

Indeed, she would not leave the water on the first full-throttle run down the lagoon, nor on the second harrowing run. Hamilton was beginning to sweat, but on the third try she staggered into the hot morning air. He headed for Midway, which they knew had been attacked. Not knowing what to expect when they arrived, because of the radio silence, and not having the slightest idea where the Japanese attackers were, Hamilton droned on to the east, flying about twenty-five feet over the water to present the smallest and least visible target he could.

They flew like that all day long, and when darkness fell at last, Hamilton lifted the clipper to a more comfortable altitude. With all the radio beacons out, they had no signal to follow, so Hamilton and his navigator, J. A. Hurtsky, relied on celestial navigation. Armed with sextants, they took star sightings at the same time, then checked their readings against each other.

They had no trouble finding Midway. It was on fire, and they could see it for miles before they arrived. Hamilton put the clipper down just above the wave tops and flew past to investigate. To his enormous relief, the defenders did not mistake him for a Japanese plane and did not fire. However, the lagoon was littered with small boats and debris, and everything seemed to be on fire. Hamilton landed as far from the burning wreckage as he could, then taxied to where he thought the Pan American dock should be. While he was taking on fuel, the ground crew told him he had just missed the shelling, which apparently came from one submarine that attacked just after dark.

Richard Boerner, a civilian construction employee working for CPNAB (Contractors Pacific Naval Air Bases) on Midway, had been on a nearby island fishing with some friends. They were told of the attack when the launch came to pick them up for lunch.

"It was hard to believe until we saw some PBYs being flown to the Dutch East Indies," he said. "Their insignias were being blacked out.

"That night a Japanese submarine came to the south end of Sand Island and fired about half a dozen five-inch shells at our hangar, where we had everything stored from the ship that had landed the day before. It was set on fire, and they knocked the corner off the power station roof.

"I was twenty-two years old at the time and had no training, and here I was lying out on the sand dunes with only a pair of shorts and tee shirt on while shells whizzed overhead.

"Finally one of the PBYs took off and dropped some depth charges on the sub. I don't know if he hit him or not, but the sub didn't fire any more.

"We got no relief until March 1942. The highest point on the island was about twenty-six feet, so there was no place to go."

This was the situation when Hamilton arrived, and he left as soon as he could, bound for Honolulu.

When he saw Oahu in the distance the next morning, he broke radio silence and asked about landing. He was given approval; by this time the nervous gunners were tired and under control, and he was not shot at as he came down onto Pearl Harbor amid the destruction. The Pan American facilities on Ford Island had not been destroyed, and two days later he flew on to San Francisco.

It was a stroke of luck that Hamilton was able to escape Wake, because not long after he left, the Japanese began bombarding the island and continued for two weeks; then, when hardly anything remained standing, they stormed ashore. A detachment of 400 Marines fought valiantly but were badly outnumbered.

(Ironically, as the war progressed, the Allies decided to ignore Wake during the island-hopping campaign of the Pacific, and the heavily fortified Japanese garrison sat for four years with absolutely nothing to do. Toward the end of the war, American submarines picked off every Japanese vessel headed to Wake with food and reinforcements. Finally the Japanese military leaders gave up on the island. Hundreds of men starved to death, and when the first Americans landed after the war ended, Wake was little more than a cemetery.)

The *Hong Kong Clipper* was the only clipper lost to the invasion. The oldest in service, it was sitting in Hong Kong Harbor and was used as a ferry between Hong Kong and Manila. When the invasion came, Captain William L. Bond was ordered to fly her to the presumed safety of Manila. But before he could get down to the harbor and crank her up, the Japanese planes came. He arrived at the dock just in time to see the Japanese using her for target practice. She burned at the dock.

The *Pacific Clipper,* on its way from one beautiful island chain (New Caledonia) to another (New Zealand), was just beginning one of the greatest sagas in commercial aviation.

When Captain Robert Ford got the news of the Pearl Harbor attack, he followed his orders: to silence the radio, to post men at windows and in the navigator's blister to watch for enemy planes, and to alter his course by fifty miles to escape any attempted interception.

When they landed in Auckland, Ford found himself more or less on his own because the cables sent in code were piling up in the cable office while the few decoding clerks struggled unsuccessfully to keep up. Ford knew he should get the flying boat home, and proceeded to do so by becoming the first commercial pilot to fly around the world.

He struck out on the 23,000-mile trip with only his crew and their tools, no navigational equipment, and only limited use of his radio. He also had to find a route that would keep them far from both the Japanese and the Germans. For navigational charts he had a collection of maps and school textbooks gathered by an employee who lived in New Zealand.

While contemplating his route home, Ford received a message from New York ordering him to pick up company personnel at Nouméa, New Caledonia. They loaded the clipper with fuel and took off late on the night of December 15.

They arrived in New Caledonia just after dawn, and Hamilton told the employees they had one hour to pack one small bag each. Now he had twenty-two more people aboard and a load of fuel. He flew to Gladstone, Australia, and went looking for fuel. Unable to find any, the crew got some sleep and took off again across the Australian desert for Darwin, flying all day across a landscape devoid of water. It was the first of several overland routes.

Darwin was in a state of panic over the war, and women and children were being evacuated. The crew refueled in the middle of a terrible thunderstorm and took off at 2 A.M. for the Dutch East Indies, where they were met by three British fighter planes that luckily held fire until they made positive identification.

They topped off the tanks with the only fuel they could get, automobile gasoline. The engines popped, backfired, and missed all the way to Ceylon, where they landed and rested at Trincomalee for a few hours. When they took off again, one of the engines finally blew and they returned to Trincomalee so the flight engineers could open up the engine and see what they could do for it. The big planes could not fly safely with one of the four engines out of service.

They could not repair the engine because a special tool they needed was not aboard. The engineers went to a British warship, borrowed some steel and a lathe, and built the tool themselves. Two days later they took off with all engines working and flew across India to Karachi—fueled with aviation gas this time—and went on to Bahrain. There they found only automobile gasoline and were told they could not fly across the Arabian Peninsula; instead, they were ordered to follow the southern border along Yemen, then on to the Red Sea.

Ford agreed; by now he would tell people whatever he thought they wanted to hear if they would let him get back into the sky. He took off and immediately headed across the barren Arabian Peninsula and over the Red Sea on a straight line to the next fuel stop in Khartoum, in the middle of Africa. They arrived safely, refueled with aviation gasoline, and headed for the Pan American base that had just been established in Leopoldville, Belgian Congo.

They left Leopoldville in perhaps the worst conditions of the entire flight. The temperature was high, and the air was so humid it seemed to drip. They were loaded with fuel, and the engines were getting very tired. They had to take off down the Congo River toward a series of rapids. Ford pushed the four throttles ahead as far as they would go and left them there. One full minute of full throttle was all the manuals permitted, but Ford had no choice; it was take off or perish. At the end of about ninety seconds, a minute longer than a normal takeoff and almost forever for a pilot or flight engineer, the clipper cleared the river.

The adventure was not over; Ford could not get the plane to lift as he roared down the Congo River gorge at full throttle, only inches from the water. He was forced to make flat turns in the twisting gorge by using only his rudders; to have banked with the ailerons would have caused the plane to hit the water. At last, after at least three minutes of the toughest flying he had ever experienced, Ford felt the lumbering clipper's controls stiffen and respond to his touch. They finally lifted clear of the gorge and the jungle, and soon were over the Atlantic, bound for Brazil.

The flight across the South Atlantic was uneventful, and they landed in Natal, Brazil, where ground crews stole everything they could find in the plane, including all the crew's money and papers. Flat broke, wearing filthy clothes, and so tired they could hardly remember their own names, they flew north to Trinidad, almost deafened by one engine that had lost its exhaust stack. They trudged on to the north, into winter in New York. As they entered New York Harbor, Ford issued a masterpiece of understatement and brevity. On January 6, 1942, thirty-one days after leaving Auckland, New Zealand, Ford radioed: "*Pacific Clipper* inbound from Auckland, New Zealand, Captain Ford reporting. Due arrive Pan American Marine Terminal LaGuardia seven minutes."

Ford brought her in for a textbook-perfect landing. Home at last. Then he ran aground on a sandbar while taxiing to the station. After a few anxious moments—to have done what he had done, then to be grounded at this point was too unfair to contemplate—Ford mentally crossed his fingers and gave the engines one last blast. The clipper slid off the sandbar and taxied majestically up to the dock. It was so cold that ice formed wherever water hit the plane, and the tiedowns were as stiff as reinforcing bar. Ford and his crew, dressed in tropical clothing, shivered so badly they could hardly talk. But the *Pacific Clipper* was home safe.

12

The Forgotten Attack

The Pearl Harbor attack has become such a symbol of the war in the Pacific that we often forget about the other attacks Japan launched simultaneously against America, Great Britain, the Philippines, Thailand, China, Malaysia, and other nations, all across the western Pacific. To those who survived them, the attacks were as devastating as that at Pearl Harbor, and only a prologue to the terrors Americans would face when the Japanese stormed ashore a few days later.

What people in Hawaii feared the most actually happened in the Philippines, on Wake and Guam, and in Hong Kong: Japanese paratroopers and infantrymen landed and quickly overran the meager American, Philippine, English, and Chinese forces.

Just after dawn on that day (because of the international date line, it was Monday, December 8, from the Philippines west) the Japanese attacked Hong Kong, first with planes that knocked out the tiny air force of three torpedo bombers and two amphibians. Then troops stationed across the border in China marched into the British territory and quickly conquered it.

On Formosa, which Japan had held since taking it from China in 1895, the bomber and fighter pilots were supposed to take off for the Philippines at sunrise in order to gain as much of a surprise as possible, although they must have known news of the Pearl Harbor attack would have reached the Philippines before dawn. However, Formosa was fogged in and the attack force had to sit on the field all morning, waiting for the fog to burn off.

This attack would bring Lieutenant General Douglas MacArthur into the war. MacArthur was one of America's most controversial military commanders because of his imperial manner and his tendency to personalize the war. With his strong profile, crumpled cap, sunglasses, and corncob pipe, he cut a dramatic figure and gave the impression he was posing for a cover of *Life* magazine. He had retired after more than thirty years in the Army and was living in the Philippines, working as a consultant to the government; but as the international tensions rose, he was called back to duty in the summer of 1941 and given command of American forces in the region.

Major General Lewis Brereton, the relatively new air commander under MacArthur at Clark Field, about fifty miles from Manila, put his forces on ready alert at 4 A.M., shortly after he had been awakened to be told of the Pearl Harbor attack (which occurred at 2:55 A.M. Manila time). He went to MacArthur's headquarters at about 5 A.M. to wait for orders. While he was there, General Henry "Hap" Arnold, commander of the Army Air Force, called Brereton and told him that whatever he did, he must not get caught with his planes on the ground, as had happened that morning in Hawaii.

Several times the fighters took off in response to false alarms and imagined sounds. Brereton repeatedly asked MacArthur for permission to attack Formosa, but MacArthur always held back, wanting to be sure the Japanese were the aggressor. MacArthur had been told by General George Marshall, in a message Brereton had hand-delivered when he reported for duty that fall, that Japan must make the first move, that it must, beyond all doubt, be the aggressor. Brereton was beside himself as his planes responded to the false alarms and his bombers were put into the air to keep them from being sitting ducks and to search the sea around Luzon for the enemy.

At about 9 A.M. Lieutenant Colonel John Horan, commander of Camp John Hay near Baguio, phoned MacArthur and said his base had been attacked. Baguio is a cool, lush mountain city in northern Luzon where the government retreated from the summer heat. MacArthur was also told that the Japanese had attacked Iba, Tuguegarao, and Tarlac. The Baguio attack came from a fleet of high-altitude bombers that demolished several buildings and killed nine people. Another attack was made on Davao City on Mindanao. Although MacArthur had been awakened at the same time as Brereton with news of the Pearl Harbor attack, he would not permit a retaliatory raid on Formosa.

Finally, at 10 A.M. the fog lifted from Formosa and the Japanese air armada headed to the Philippines. At 11 A.M. MacArthur decided Brereton was right and authorized him to attack Formosa. Unfortunately it was too late, and the Japanese had another run of luck. The American planes had been airborne most of the morning, searching for the attackers and trying to avoid being caught on the ground. Now that they had permission to go to war, they were not armed with bombs and did not have enough fuel to fly to Formosa and back. They landed at Clark Field to be refueled and armed. While the ground crews were busy doing this, the plane crews went into the mess hall for lunch in a high state of excitement. War at last!

Meanwhile, the main fleet of Japanese fighters and bombers was on the way to Clark Field, their progress reported all along the route by radar screens and people on the ground. Postmasters in small Philippine villages were telegraphing or telephoning Clark Field about the large number of planes headed their way, and the radar operators did the same.

Bob Paradise was an Army surgical technician stationed in Manila since 1938. He was due to leave for the mainland on December 8 or 9, aboard a ship that was berthed in Manila harbor. On that morning he and a friend were in downtown Manila when they heard the air-raid sirens. They went out into the street and saw the flocks of planes flying overhead, bound for the harbor.

"My friend and I jumped into a cab and told the driver to take us to the harbor," Paradise said. "When we got our first view of the harbor, the first thing I saw—my eyes were like a zoom lens, I think—was the ship burning. She had taken two bombs right down the stack, and there went my transportation home.

"Instead, I was reassigned and automatically reenlisted for the duration of the war. I was captured on Bataan and was a prisoner of war for forty-six months. I often wonder what changes would have been in my life if my home-bound ship had not been bombed that day."

No satisfactory explanation has been given why these warnings were so completely unheeded or why none of the warnings got through to the bomber command. The big planes sat on the runway, dumb as water buffaloes. Only the fighter squadrons around the islands were notified, and most of them were refueled, armed, and in the air searching for the enemy while protecting the various airfields. The B-17s just sat there.

At 11:45 A.M. a pursuit squadron at Clark Field prepared to take off. The P-40s got into the air, but the older, slower P-35s were held up by a windstorm that blew thick dust across the runways. At about 12:15 they taxied out again to take off, just as the first bombs fell from high-altitude bombers. Only three or four of the P-35s got off the ground; at least five were blown up on the runway.

The Japanese bombers and fighters were preceded by scout planes that circled the peaceful airport unchallenged for perhaps ten minutes before the slower bombers arrived. Below them were 21 of the 35 B-17s and many of the fighters. Almost exactly ten hours after the Pearl Harbor attack, the Japanese planes descended on Clark Field. The bombers were very accurate—"the most accurate bombing I ever witnessed by our own planes," wrote one of the Japanese pilots—demolishing most of the American bombers and many of the hangars. The fighters were equally accurate and shot down most of the P-40s that were struggling to get off the ground and into battle. The carnage went on for about an hour. When the Japanese were finally forced by low fuel to return to Formosa, they left behind 18 destroyed B-17s and 53 (of 107) fighters. Their losses were seven Zeros and no bombers. Fourteen B-17s escaped the attack because they were 600 miles away on Mindanao.

General "Hap" Arnold's greatest fear was realized: The bulk of his fleet of bombers and fighters was parked on the ground and destroyed. Unlike his counterparts in Hawaii, General MacArthur was never formally accused of an error in judgment. He was as unprepared for the attack as General Short and Admiral Kimmel, but no official reprimand was issued. If anything, he was treated as a victim of the Japanese while his counterparts in Hawaii were treated as if they had conspired with the enemy.

13

On the Home Front

In mainland America the day began innocently enough: a calm Sunday at the end of autumn. Football season was almost over, and most high school athletes were glad, because they were tired of being tackled on the frozen, cleat-marked ground. Basketball in the heated, crowded gymnasium was something to look forward to.

The weather was dry and sunny throughout most of the country, although people in Norfolk, Virginia, complained that it was the coldest day of the year. Perhaps the coldest city in the country was Chicago, which reported a temperature of 37 degrees with a strong wind off Lake Michigan.

All across America, Christmas decorations hung from lamp posts and adorned store windows, and municipal Christmas trees had been decorated and lit in squares and public parks. A few homes had a decorated tree in front of the living room window, but most families would wait until two weeks before Christmas to get a tree. Many families would make their own decorations: strings of berries and popcorn on heavy thread, paper chains, popcorn balls, stars or other figures of cardboard covered with tinfoil, and perhaps a store-bought angel for the top of the tree.

Most families would rise a little later than on the other six days, and breakfast would be later and less organized. Some fathers and children would prepare their own breakfasts and eat in silence while reading their favorite sections of the newspaper. Some would listen to the Mormon Tabernacle Choir on the radio. Children reading the backs of cereal boxes were likely to find military aircraft identification kits, biographies of famous military and sports personalities, and some of the cutout buildings from the Lone Ranger village that they could acquire if their parents bought three or four more boxes of the same cereal. If parents had made a particularly bad choice of cereal, they would be forced to read about good nutrition.

Some couples, particularly those without children, would prepare breakfast, put it on a tray, and eat in bed while reading the paper. One of the favorite newspaper stories that morning was an account of the breakup of the fifth marriage of Thomas Franklyn Manville, Jr. The union ended on Saturday, after only seventeen days. Tommy Manville was one of America's favorite husbands, and each of the forty-seven-year-old asbestos millionaire's marriages and subsequent divorces was national news. Most of his weddings and divorces were relatively lighthearted affairs, but this one was different. Tommy really cared about this wife, and one sensed that he might stay single a long time after this divorce, or he might stay married a long time if he did remarry again.

His fifth marriage was to thirty-two-year-old Bonita Edwards, a showgirl. The others had been showgirls, too, except his second wife, who had been his father's secretary. His first marriage had lasted eleven years, the second five years, the third six months, the fourth four years.

"It was just incompatibility," Bonita told a reporter.

"We got along fine," Manville told another reporter. He did admit, though, that one of his ex-wives might have been a factor, because she kept calling to insist on the $3,200 she said she was owed in back alimony.

Manville ushered Bonita aboard the train, along with her mother, her brother, two attorneys, and two reporters. Then he left the train and stood watching it pull away. He told reporters that when his other wives had left, he was "tickled to death. This time I'm not."

One of the oddest stories involved a steeplejack named L. T. Hill, who fell from a hundred-foot church tower in Ellsworth, Wisconsin. On the way down he struck two projections, skittered off a slanting roof, and landed on a concrete sidewalk.

"He got up and strode off, nursing a sore thumb while a doctor and an undertaker looked on with whatever feelings a doctor and an undertaker would have under the amazing circumstances."

Military terms had been popping up in newspapers since the late 1930s, on the comics pages, and in automobile ads. Subscribers to the *Daily Oklahoman* read a story about a new portable X-ray unit that was being hauled all over the state in a trailer in the effort to diagnose and eradicate tuberculosis. The headline said "State's War on Tuberculosis Moves at Blitzkrieg Pace." An ad for a book sale called it a "bookskreig," and one automobile agency called its new car a "B-44."

The comics pages also reflected the militaristic tone of the period. Flash Gordon was in trouble because he had stolen a seaplane from the unnamed enemy in the Pacific and was shot down by friendly fire. The plane did not carry the Rising Sun on the side, but the insignia was circular and looked very similar to those of Japanese patrol planes.

In "Bringing Up Father," Jiggs was astounded at the amount of clothes Maggie bought for their vacation, but of course it was easy for Maggie to astound Jiggs; he lived in a perpetual state of astonishment.

The Oklahoma City transportation systems were bracing themselves for a major influx (newspaper headline writers restrained themselves from calling it an invasion) of soldiers going home on Christmas leave. More than a quarter of a million soldiers stationed in Oklahoma, Texas, Arkansas, Louisiana, and New Mexico were scheduled to go home for Christmas, and Oklahoma City was one of the hub cities for trains and buses. Empty buses and railroad cars were being sent to the depots nearest the camps, to be available when the holiday leaves began around December 13.

A similar influx of servicemen caused traffic jams in Rhode Island because 22,000 soldiers in 3,400 vehicles were on their way back to Camp Edwards from maneuvers in the Carolinas; one convoy would go through Providence at noon on Saturday. The *Providence Sunday Journal* devoted several pages to military subjects. One page was given over to the military public relations staff to fill with pleasant chit-chat and folksy items about enlisted men, something on the order of what Bill Mauldin would later make famous during the war.

For example, "Pvt. Al Cantara of Pawtucket is known as 'Dogface.' Probably because he sleeps in a pup-tent, wears a dogtag for identification and is always growling about something or other."

Studebaker's 1942 Commander Land Cruiser was selling for $1,243 in Denver. For the most part, the new automobiles advertised on December 7 would be the same automobiles advertised in 1945 and 1946 when the manufacturers stopped building jeeps, tanks, airplanes, and other military products and returned to automobiles, using the equipment that went into storage in 1941.

Unemployment was the lowest in more than a decade; the average weekly wage was now $29.58 ($1,538 a year), but 27 percent of Americans were earning only $420 a year. Nutritionists said it cost $150 a year to feed one person adequately, or $600 for a family of four. A complete dinner cost 75 cents at the Manhattan Restaurant at 1635 Larimer Street in Denver, with a choice of steak, chicken, mountain trout, or Louisiana frog legs.

Potatoes cost 19 cents for 10 pounds in Seattle. Butter was 37 cents a pound, ground beef 20 cents a pound, oranges a penny each, and eggs 41 cents a dozen. Firewood cost $8 a cord, coffee was 30 cents a pound, and you could rent a room with hot water, heat, and a private bathroom for $3 a week. Electrolux vacuum cleaners were selling for $15.95, with all attachments, and a three-piece bedroom set could be bought for $44.95.

Newspapers were running military-related fillers. One which appeared in several papers on December 7 reported that more than 12,168,000 eggs and 55,000,000 pounds of fruit would be consumed by Navy personnel during the next year. Another filler described the stainless steel trays sailors ate from, and went on to tell how they were washed.

The competition between Colorado and Texas over size was fueled by a claim made by the Colorado tourism officials that Colorado was actually larger than Texas. This claim was made on mathematical computations which showed that there was more of Colorado above sea level than there was of Texas. Multiplying Colorado's 103,948 square miles by its mean altitude of 6,800 feet (1.287 miles) gave the state 133,872 cubic miles, compared with only 72,837 cubic miles for Texas.

In retrospect it seems perfectly obvious that war was coming and that America would have a role in it. For example, the Curtiss-Wright plant which opened in Columbus, Ohio, that week was the largest dive-bomber plant in America. Also, the Navy announced it was easing its physical standards and would accept into all branches except the Marine Corps men who were suffering from varicose veins, hernia, and hydrocele; the Marines would accept some men with varicose veins.

The defense industry had been hiring more and more jobless men or those on publicly funded programs such as the Works Progress Administration (WPA) and the Civilian Conservation Corps. In some cases, projects those agencies were undertaking had to be canceled or delayed due to the labor shortage—for instance, a playground project in the Georgiaville area of Providence, Rhode Island, that had been funded with $1,200 from the WPA. The *Providence Journal* noted that no workers in town were on the WPA rolls.

In other news, royalty watchers read that King Leopold III of Belgium had taken a commoner bride. His previous queen had died in an automobile accident. The marriage had occurred secretly two months earlier in London, where the monarch was sitting out the war after his dreams of neutrality were ignored by Germany when its armies swept into Belgium. Other Belgian exiles in England were less than enthusiastic about the wedding and the secrecy surrounding it.

The first major war news most of us heard on the radio on December 7 was England's reluctant declaration of war against Finland, Hungary, and Romania the previous day. Most of the other international news broadcasts were about the war in Europe and the tension that existed between the United States and Japan. The CBS anchorman in the New York newsroom that day was John Charles Daly, and at noon he gave a brief rundown of the day's general news, including a report that the Germans had broken through some of the Russian lines, and that Russia was claiming it had broken through Nazi lines at two points, overrunning two divisions. Then he began calling in correspondents: Bob Trout from London, Ford Wilkins from Manila, and Albert Warner from Washington.

Wilkins said that preparations for war had reached a new level in the Philippines and that all Navy personnel had been recalled to their ships and all Air Force men ordered to their barracks.

Albert Warner said that Washington was maintaining a grim silence. "Washington is not convinced that the Japanese note regarding troop movements delivered on Saturday was honest." The note delivered on December 6 claimed that Japan was reinforcing its troops in northern French Indochina (now Vietnam) "with the object of taking precautionary measures" against Chinese troops along its border. Later it was learned that on that same day Japan and Germany had signed a secret treaty for a war against the United States that also prevented either from agreeing to a separate peace.

Warner said that nobody in Washington seemed upset that England had declared war on Finland—he hardly mentioned Hungary and Romania—and he cited one report that America would seize Finnish ships in American waters.

Warner did not report, but newspaper correspondents did, what Finland's President Risto Ryti said about the situation. He reminded the world that his people were simply fighting back against Russia, which had attacked them over disputed territory. This was a quarrel that predated Hitler's Germany and should have had no effect on England and America, since Finland had no quarrel whatsoever with them. President Ryti's dislike for the Russians was well known, but at the moment he thought even less of Hitler. When Russia took advantage of the situation and attacked Finland, it left the small country no choice but to side with someone else fighting Russia.

Then President Ryti made one of the most prophetic statements of the period: "Russia's friendships with the United States and Great Britain are a leper's handicap."

Secretary of the Navy Frank Knox contributed some sword rattling for the weekend newspapers and radio broadcasts by saying America was the greatest power in the world, "but we must arm against any possible combinations of powers against us." He noted that 325 ships had been christened, 2,059 airplanes had been acquired, 700 vessels were under construction, and Navy personnel had been increased by 15,000 officers and men. He said that the air bases in the Aleutian Islands and on the Alaskan mainland had a strategic importance that was obvious. He also said that the entire stock of fuel oil in Hawaii would eventually be stored underground.

Secretary Knox's report was quoted at great length, citing the many bases America had strung across the Pacific, one of which was only 1,500 miles from Japan. The eventual goal was to have 17 battleships, 6 carriers, 208 heavy cruisers and destroyers, and 113 submarines patrolling in what the Navy called the Two Ocean program.

The Army had 29 regular and 4 armored divisions with a total of 1.6 million officers and men, more than double the troop strength a year earlier. The goal was to have 3 million men wearing Army uniforms. The Army Air Force had 167,000 men and about 3,000 combat planes, with the B-17 bomber and the P-40 fighter the mainstays. To meet these goals, Congress had just authorized a stunning $74.4 billion defense budget.

One newspaper commentator who had nothing to be embarrassed about on December 8 was Constantine Brown, a columnist syndicated by the George Matthew Adams Service, out of Washington, D.C. His assessment of the situation was blunt: "The chances of avoiding a conflict in the Pacific are now so slim that diplomatic gamblers are giving odds of 100 to 1 in favor of war with Japan and 10 to 1 that it breaks out before the end of the year.

"From the latest exchanges of views between American officials and the Japanese negotiators, Ambassador Nomura and Saburo Kurusu, it is evident that the Japanese have definitely made up their minds to risk a war with the ABCD powers.

"The only reason for their continuance of negotiations with the United States it to give their navy and army general staffs time to concentrate the forces which are being sent south, either from home bases or various parts of China."

The accuracy of his predictions was being proven at the moment many people were reading his comments.

A *Washington Post* columnist, Edward T. Folliard, was not so fortunate. He had written in that day's paper that as long as the diplomats kept talking, the average American "refuses to become terribly excited. His attitude is something like that of John L. Sullivan when he was heavyweight champion and lesser men were trying to pick a fight with him. The Boston Strong Boy, with justifiable hauteur, used to tell them, 'Go get a reputation.' "

That paragraph was still haunting Folliard in 1971 when he wrote an article on the thirtieth anniversary of the attack: "Well," he wrote ruefully, "Japan had a reputation now."

Rear Admiral Clark H. Woodward, a columnist for the International News Service, wrote an especially upbeat column for the Sunday papers, saying among other things that the British were on a strong Libyan offensive as good as anything the Germans had ever mounted. When he spoke of the Pacific tension, he noted that the Nipponese military apparatus was made up of inferior fighters and that the trade restrictions imposed by America, including the closing of the Panama Canal, spelled doom for Japan.

In the *Daily Oklahoman* a reporter named Kay Park began a three-part series on the effect the defense buildup was having on the University of Oklahoma campus. Her first article captured the mood of that day as well as anything written or spoken on the subject: "Rumbles from a war which roars thousands of miles away are rolling in increasing volume over the tree-lined borders of this easy-going campus, leaving in their wake a disturbing question mark on life at the University of Oklahoma.

"Old men talk and threaten, but it is the boys of college age who will whip Hitler, if he is whipped, and the tremendous national defense effort is something close and personal to students here. . . .

"Joe College is dead, perhaps forever, and in his place is a serious young man torn with doubt as to the part he should take in a seething world crisis.

"Every day troubled students crowd the office of Fayette Copeland, counselor for men, trying to find the answer. . . . The number of students planning to quit school has increased rapidly the last few weeks, with the growing seriousness of the international picture."

In other news around the hemisphere, the coal mine dispute was expected to end within forty-eight hours, and the Labor Board, including John L. Lewis, would meet again Monday.

Cuba's dictator, Colonel Fulgencio Batista, had asked his congress to declare an emergency so he could rule by decree for forty-five days in order to work on the nation's defense.

Mexico announced a plan by Nazis to explode ships in Tampico harbor, in an effort to destroy the entire harbor, and Honduras said the Axis had planned to set up puppet governments in Latin America to fight against the United States.

Shortly after a report that Argentina was preparing for an election and that all its troops had been confined to barracks and planes grounded to prevent the possibility of disturbances, most radio stations broadcasting news went momentarily silent as the newsmen absorbed the enormity of bulletins from Honolulu and Manila.

14

War Comes to the Football Game

If it is possible to point to an instant when everything changed, then 7:55 A.M. Honolulu time was such an instant. It was 10:25 on the West Coast, 11:25 in the Rocky Mountains, 12:25 in the Midwest, and 1:25 on the East Coast. History paused for a heartbeat, stumbled, then resumed its measured pace. America no longer had its innocence. It was the new, reluctant member of the nonexclusive club of nations that had been attacked by a foreign power.

One of the first broadcasts of the news came from NBC, which read an announcement from its affiliate KGU, in Honolulu. Across America radio programs were interrupted to announce the attack. Many people remember listening to Shostakovich's First Symphony being played by the New York Philharmonic when they first heard the news. An announcer broke in, then the orchestra continued playing the Russian's tense, sometimes strident music. On the West Coast the three major networks were broadcasting "Chicago Round Table" (NBC Red), "The World Today" (CBS), and "Swingtime Strings" (Mutual). Unaffiliated stations were carrying religious programs or professional football games.

The Honolulu correspondent was reasonably calm in his announcement:

"We have witnessed this morning the attack of Pearl Harbor and the severe bombing of Pearl Harbor by army planes that are undoubtedly Japanese. The city of Honolulu has also been attacked and considerable damage done. This battle has been going on for nearly three hours. One of the bombers dropped within fifty feet of Tanti Towers. It's no joke—

it's a real war. The public of Honolulu has been advised to keep in their homes and away from the Army and Navy. There has been severe fighting going on in the air and on the sea."

For the first time in history, America had been attacked by a foreign power, and nobody knew quite what to make of it.

The radio newsmen quickly regained their composure and began what they knew would be a grueling few days with hardly any sleep or rest, and minutes and hours of airtime to fill with commentary when there was not necessarily much to comment on. As in all situations, there were moments of brilliance and moments the reporters later wished they could erase from history.

A widely published and quoted military expert, Major George Fielding Elliott, went on the air and said, among other things, that "It should be emphasized that this attack is of a suicidal nature from which few of the ships' aircraft and personnel participating have any hope of returning. It is a procedure entirely in keeping with the Japanese character."

Many movie theaters ran announcements across the bottom of the screen, if they had the capability of doing so, and some interrupted the film to give the news. Many did not bother, if they knew of the attack at all. Thus, most moviegoers did not know about the attack until the films were over.

One of the most popular movies that month was *Sergeant York,* the biographical film of America's reluctant World War I hero, portrayed by Gary Cooper. A reporter from the *Chattanooga Times* drove out to York's home in the mountains to see what he thought of the attack.

"We got to put up a united front and give those folks a lickin' right away," he was quoted as saying. "We should take care of the Japs first and then take on the Germans."

The people of America did what people and other species of animals do whenever the entire community is threatened: They huddled together—in their homes, in hotel lobbies, in restaurants. They needed the comfort of others, and everywhere people went out on their front porches, on the lawns or the sidewalks to talk to friends and neighbors, always within earshot of a radio in a car or in the house, often with a window open so they would not miss any part of the news.

Direct-dial telephones did not exist then, and every call had to be placed through an operator. On that day the operators were swamped with calls and extra operators were called to work. In Montgomery, Alabama, the operators were not nearly as busy as the day Carole Lombard was killed in a plane crash. On that day the telephone system had almost self-destructed as fuses blew, one after another.

Jean Godden was a grade schooler living in Oakland, California. Her family and another family from the Presbyterian church went on a picnic that afternoon in the mountains near Marin. For her birthday in October, Jean had been given a portable radio, an item that was not very common then. Hers was about the size of a modern clock radio and made of Bakelite plastic. It had a little door that was opened to turn it on, and it used enormous batteries. Their car did not have a radio—few cars did then—so she took it along.

When the picnic—fried chicken and potato salad—was laid out on the table, she turned on the radio.

"We heard 'The Japanese have just bombed Pearl Harbor,' and that was all. The radio died. It stopped right at that moment, and it never made another sound. We took it to repair shops several times, and nobody could ever get it to work."

Hal Kosut was an announcer on duty at radio station WPAT in Paterson, New Jersey, that afternoon. He did not have much to do at that time of day because the station was broadcasting a local football game with Steve Ellis as the sportscaster.

"Suddenly I heard the tinkling of the bells on our radio wire-service machine, indicating a news bulletin," Kosut remembers. "Rushing over to the machine, I read with consternation the awful news. I ripped off the bulletin, instructed the control engineer to phase out of the ball game and broadcast the bulletin. After promising our listeners further details as they came in, I had the game resumed.

"The initial announcement by Steve Ellis, who was later to serve with distinction on ABC Radio, knocked me for a loop. In a matter-of-fact manner he said, 'Okay. The Japs have attacked. Now back to the ball game.' "

Donald E. Forrer was recently married and working part time in the advertising department of Pan American Airways Systems. One of his jobs was making minor alterations, such as route changes, as needed on the several wall maps in the traffic managers' and vice presidents' offices.

When news of the attack came, newspaper reporters showed up at the office in the Chrysler Building because of Pan American's worldwide routes and because they knew Pan American would have planes in the war zone. Indeed, it had four giant clippers scattered across the Pacific. Also, Juan Trippe had turned the airline into an American showcase. The words "Pan American" came to be a symbol of American strength and imagination for Americans and foreigners alike. In the minds of many Americans, Pan American was an extension of American policy, and we tended to think of the airline as being part of the government without really being subject to its restrictions. Nobody was surprised to hear that Secretary of War Knox had called Juan Trippe as soon as he could, to tell him of the attack. Trippe went down to the office to speak to the reporters and to see what could be done for his planes.

With all the confusion in the office, Forrer couldn't work, so he was sent home.

"In my apartment nearby, my young wife and I pored over charts and we found one: The Territory of Hawaii and Honolulu Town. But we failed to find Pearl Harbor [on it]."

In California, Virginia and Bill Scott, who had been married only a few weeks, invited another couple to join them at their cabin in the desert near March Air Force Base, in the Riverside area.

"We were hunting jackrabbits and playing soldier with our husbands, guns over their shoulders and we wives marching behind. Suddenly we were aware of an airplane buzzing us, two or three times, then it flew off. It struck us as strange. Only later that afternoon, when we were driving home, did we hear on the radio, 'U.S. at war with Japan.' I guess our innocent little marching with the guns was suspect."

Bob Meek, a fourteen-year-old freshman at San Mateo, California, Union High, was working on weekends as a caddy at the local golf course.

"I was packing a 'double' for two golfers, and as we came off the front nine, I noticed some action at the little hot dog stand outside the clubhouse. The two golfers went on to the back nine, so it was about two hours later that I got back to the hot dog stand, where a radio was on.

"The other caddies said Pearl Harbor had been bombed, and the news over the radio was adding such details as were known and the fact that this meant war.

"My very first response was, 'Oh shucks! It will all be over before I can get in.' I did get in at the tail end of the war but never got out of California."

All across America, Orientals felt their blood chill when they heard the news. Japanese Americans were especially concerned because they knew they would be categorized simply as Japs. One Japanese-American boy who was in high school had been given the use of the family car that day and was taking his sister and one of her girlfriends for a ride around Seattle. He knew something was wrong when they were greeted everywhere with sullen stares, because before "people always looked right through us as if we didn't exist."

In the Phoenix area many residents were worried about sabotage because at least a thousand Japanese Americans farmed in the Salt River Valley. Armed guards had been placed on the Salt River dams for the past several months.

Before dark the FBI and other federal agencies were already talking about rounding up Japanese Americans. In San Diego County, where some two thousand lived, the Japanese Americans were staying off the streets as much as possible and, when asked by reporters, insisted they were loyal to America.

Everywhere Chinese and Filipino residents worried about the reaction of Caucasians who could easily mistake them for Japanese. Most merchants immediately put up signs stating their nationality, and some called the police and newspapers to seek help in avoiding confusion. Pittsburgh had a very small Chinatown that covered approximately a block, and most of its citizens were out on the street shaking hands with each other and laughing gleefully because their homeland would at last be defended by America.

Paul McCurdy was a junior high school principal in Auburn, a small town near Seattle. Two boys in the eighth grade lived on the same block as he did, and that morning he was out in the street throwing and kicking a football with them.

"All of a sudden the door of a neighbor's house flew open, and he came bursting out into his yard and announced to the whole east side of town, 'The Japs are attacking Pearl Harbor and are blasting everything to pieces.'

"Of course everyone outside his own home lit for home and kept an ear to the radio for many hours. I went outside once to see if anyone was moving, and there was a dreadful silence—no sound at all. The air was absolutely quiet. I'm sure I never will forget that moment. (I am quite adept at forgetting lots of things these days.)"

Among his students were more than a hundred Japanese Americans, who, like all Japanese Americans living within a hundred miles of the western coastline, would soon be rounded up with their parents and sent to relocation camps in Montana, Idaho, Wyoming, Utah, Arizona, Colorado, and as far east as Arkansas.

Jean West noticed the same thing that evening in Washington, D.C. A teacher, she had spent the afternoon correcting papers and working on lesson plans without the radio on.

"When we went out for dinner at a coffee shop, we were amazed at the silence; no music and no conversation. Our waitress told us what happened.

"We were sure Washington would be bombed soon, and we walked home through the dark streets in a state of near panic."

Armandi Robinson went to his job that afternoon as pinsetter at a bowling alley at Broad and Spruce streets in Philadelphia. He heard of the attack while shooting pool, and continued playing pool all afternoon because nearly everyone stayed home to listen to the radio.

Jean and George McCulloch were visiting her sister and brother-in-law on Vashon Island in Puget Sound that Sunday. The McCullochs decided to go sailing in a tiny boat called a Moth that was only eight feet long and barely large enough for two people.

"We were enjoying ourselves when suddenly the wind stopped and we were becalmed. Then we realized we'd forgotten the paddle. Our friends on shore were hollering that the Japanese were bombing Pearl Harbor, but they had no other boat to come and get us."

The McCullochs could only sit and watch their friends become smaller and smaller, and finally disappear from view as the little boat was swept along in the strong tidal currents of South Puget Sound.

"As we drifted silently to the south, we hoped we wouldn't be heading for the Tacoma Narrows [a particularly dangerous stretch of water with swift tidal currents and resulting whirlpools]. We did find a piece of board floating by and used that to paddle, finally reaching shore near Gig Harbor, where we beached the boat and trudged into town in the darkness.

"A bus to Tacoma, a street car to Point Defiance, and a ferry to Tahlequah [on Vashon Island], and we were home again about eleven o'clock that night. Naturally our family was frantic and had even called the Coast Guard. My sister often asked why we didn't telephone along the way, but we were too busy trying to get back to the island."

If the Japanese and Germans had wanted to really cripple America, they would have bombed Griffith Stadium in Washington, D.C., where 27,102 fans were watching the Washington Redskins beat the Philadelphia Eagles 20 to 14 in the final game of the season. Redskin games were a major social event, and many of the most powerful government and military figures were at the game.

In the press box with several other reporters was Pat O'Brien of the Associated Press. With him was a telegrapher who sent his stories to the office in Morse code. During the game the telegrapher handed O'Brien a message from the AP bureau: "Keep it short" (meaning O'Brien's story on the game).

A few minutes later another message came, an explanation of why the game had lost some of its importance: "The Japanese have kicked off. War now."

Soon the stadium announcer began calling out names and titles: "The resident commissioner of the Philippines, Mr. Joaquin M. Elizalde, is urged to call his office at once."

"Admiral W. A. P. Blandy is asked to report to his office at once."

A steady stream of similar people were called away from the game, but no explanation was given to the fans. Jack Espy, general manager of the Redskins, later explained that they knew what had happened but did not want to "contribute to any hysteria."

Among the fans who left the game in ignorance was a twenty-four-year-old Navy ensign named John Fitzgerald Kennedy.

Another game being played in New York City was stopped.

"I was playing in a hockey game against the Manhattan Arrows, and suddenly in the middle of a rush the ref blew his whistle and we all stopped," said the Reverend William A. Spurrier. "The public address announcer said, 'Ladies and gentlemen, the Japanese have bombed Pearl Harbor. I repeat, the Japanese have bombed Pearl Harbor.'

"The lights dimmed and the organist played 'The Star Spangled Banner.' Aghast, solemn, and silent, we ended the game, went off the ice to the dressing room. After a few serious remarks about 'joining up' and wondering what to do, we all went home." Spurrier became a chaplain in the 69th Infantry Division.

Frank Waldrop, managing editor of the *Washington Times Herald,* happened to be in the office that Sunday, as he often was, to take care of paperwork without constant interruptions. When he finished his chores, he wandered back to the wire service room, more out of curiosity than anything else.

He saw a dispatch from Reuters about two Japanese battleships being seen going south in the Gulf of Siam and decided, "What the hell. Things are at a flash point now. I believe I'll stick around awhile."

About two o'clock an editor on the city desk, Tom Stephens, came rushing into Waldrop's office, his face ashen, and said he had heard a police radio report that the Japanese had bombed Pearl Harbor. Waldrop told him to call the White House for a confirmation, and he put the telephone operators to work finding key staff members.

"Fortunately all of our circulation people were out at the Redskins football game," he said. "They had some junket that the kids had wanted to attend, so there was a big crowd of them out there. I called the Redskins office and told them to put on their loudspeaker 'All *Times Herald* people report to their office on the double,' and about the same time the Navy was calling and the Army was calling, so I didn't have any problem.

"A great many printers were out there, by good chance. I also got hold of the head of the composing room, and the people who heard it on the radio didn't have to be told. They got the hell down there. So by the time the people made it to the office, I had a story and I had gotten a full description of the attack officially, including the losses and all, quite detailed."

To Waldrop's delight, the *Times Herald*'s extra edition was on the street in only four hours.

Some radio networks got the news from their correspondents and from the news agencies such as United Press, Associated Press, and International News Service. Most heard it first from President Roosevelt's press secretary, Steve Early, at 2:35 P.M. Washington time, almost exactly an hour after the first wave of Japanese planes struck Pearl Harbor.

Louise Hackmeister, superintendent of the White House switchboard, rang the three press associations and put them on a conference hookup.

"This is Steve Early at the White House," they heard. "At 7:55 A.M., Hawaiian time, the Japanese bombed Pearl Harbor. The attacks are continuing."

This set off a flurry of "flash" bells on wire machines all over America, some falling on deaf ears at newspapers that were not staffed on Sunday afternoon.

Then reports began filtering in about other attacks: the Philippines,

Guam, Wake Island, Hong Kong. These received less attention, even though American lives were lost. The Philippines was far away. So was Hong Kong. Very few Americans knew anything about these places, or particularly cared.

15

The Delayed Message

The first news of the attack had come to Washington indirectly when the naval station at Mare Island in San Francisco Bay picked up a radio message from Admiral Husband E. Kimmel, Commander in Chief, Pacific Fleet, (CINCPAC) at Pearl Harbor: FROM CINCPAC TO ALL SHIPS PRESENT IN HAWAIIAN AREA: AIR RAID ON PEARL HARBOR. THIS IS NO DRILL.

The message reached the Navy Department at 1:45 P.M. A communications officer raced over to the office of Admiral Harold R. Stark, Chief of Naval Operations, and he in turn caught Secretary of the Navy Frank Knox, who was just leaving with Rear Admiral R. K. Turner for a visit to the Washington Navy Yard.

The admiral handed the message to Knox without comment and stood by silently as he read it.

"What does it mean?" Knox asked.

"It's the beginning," Stark told him.

Turner was more specific. After he looked over Knox's shoulder to read the message, he growled, "By God, sir, they've attacked us!"

"My God," Knox said. "This can't be true. They must mean the Philippines."

Nobody knows if Knox thought of it then or not, but virtually every major newspaper in America that morning carried his story on the Navy's advanced state of preparedness in the event of war. But he did know immediately that he had to bear part of the blame for the surprise attack, and before the day was over he would tell the President he was flying to Honolulu to see the extent of the damage.

He dashed back into his office and called President Roosevelt. At that time the President was relaxing after a busy week of dealing with the crisis in the Pacific, the war in Europe, and a sinus infection. He had set aside this Sunday to relax and perhaps work on his neglected stamp collection. He was sitting in the Oval Office with a luncheon tray on his lap, chatting with his most trusted friend, Harry L. Hopkins.

Hopkins was one of the most brilliant and loyal men Roosevelt had attracted to his staff. Men who are willing to submerge their personalities and personal power at least temporarily in favor of someone else's goals are rare, especially when they are as brilliant as Hopkins. Hopkins was totally loyal and one of the most capable men in Washington, D.C., at that time, and certainly one of the most powerful. He could have had almost any office in the Roosevelt administration he wanted. But he was in poor health, and while he was recuperating from a heart attack, Roosevelt had him moved into the White House as a permanent guest.

Hopkins apparently was the only man Roosevelt trusted without reservation, and that was because he had never tried to use his office or their friendship for personal gain. In his book about the Roosevelt and Hopkins friendship, Robert Sherwood gave the example of what invariably happened when Roosevelt had some old political friends in to play cards. Sometime during the evening nearly every one of the guests would bring up a pet project in an effort to sway the President. Harry Hopkins had no projects other than those Roosevelt gave him, and Roosevelt knew that. That did not mean Hopkins was a yes-man to the President; on the contrary, he was totally honest with the President, and when he did not agree with him—which was often—he told Roosevelt so. That independence, coupled with his brilliance and total lack of personal ambition, made him more valuable to Roosevelt than anyone in his cabinet.

Roosevelt sent Hopkins all over Europe on sensitive missions that normally would have been entrusted to senior diplomats or cabinet officers such as the Secretary of State or the Secretary of War. Hopkins had a delicate antenna for what Roosevelt would want in each situation that arose, so it was he who went to Russia because Roosevelt knew that he could not be bullied and, if necessary, would call Stalin's bluff. It was Hopkins who called on Churchill and strengthened Anglo-American ties while refusing to commit America to the war.

Hopkins was born in Sioux City, Iowa, in 1890 and came to Washington in the early 1930s, after college and a career as a New York City social worker. While serving as director of New York State's relief agency, he came to the attention of Roosevelt, and in 1935 Roosevelt put him in charge of the Works Progress Administration (WPA), one of the President's most beleaguered agencies. Hopkins took his lumps on that job, including being accused of using the WPA to further the Democratic Party's goals. If Hopkins worried about such accusations, he did not show it. Next he served from 1938 until 1940 as Secretary of Commerce. In 1941 he took over another political hot potato, President Roosevelt's Lend-Lease program. By this time he was living in the White House.

He pursued each job given him without concern for political expediency. He was Roosevelt's lightning rod and did not care what anybody said about him.

On Sunday, Hopkins strolled down to the Oval Office to join Roosevelt at lunch. They were chatting about nothing in particular, with the President's famous Scottie, Fala, at their feet, when the phone rang in spite of a "Do Not Disturb" sign Roosevelt had asked them to place on his line at the switchboard.

The operator apologized but said that Secretary Knox was insisting it was urgent that he speak to the President. Roosevelt cut short the operator's apologies and told her to put Knox on the line. He said later he was always impressed with the calm and clear tone of Knox's voice when he said, "Mr. President, it looks like the Japanese have attacked Pearl Harbor."

"No!" the President shouted.

"It's true. I'll read you the message," Knox said.

Roosevelt listened, nodded, and began issuing orders to Knox to see that our bases in Alaska were being protected, and that guards at the Panama Canal were doubled.

Roosevelt hung up and told Hopkins what he had just heard.

"This is it," Hopkins said. Roosevelt next placed a call to Secretary of State Cordell Hull, who was in his office preparing for a scheduled 2 P.M. meeting with the Japanese ambassador, Admiral Kichisaburo Nomura, and the "peace envoy," Saburo Kurusu, a former resident of the United States who had been planted in Washington, D.C., by the Japanese government to be sure the scenario of the attack was carried out properly.

Most Americans believed Kurusu knew of the coming attack but that Nomura did not, suspicions that were confirmed after the war. However, it would be unfair to make Kurusu the complete villain of the situation, because he did try informally, through diplomatic channels, to convince Hull that war with Japan need not be inevitable. He went to at least two diplomatic friends and asked them to intercede with Hull. One friend was Ferdinand L. Mayer, a former U.S. ambassador to Peru whom he

which included Fort Shafter, and took off on his motorcycle. Since the message to General Short was not marked "Priority," Fuchikami went about his business as usual. He sorted the messages, dropped off one at a doctor's office on the way to Fort Shafter, and may have had others to deliver on the way.

He had not been gone long before the war began. Fuchikami kept going in spite of the bombing and strafing by Japanese planes, and the monumental traffic jams. He was stopped at a roadblock by the National Guard, who urged him to give up his mission and go home. He was wearing a green shirt and khaki trousers, and the Guardsmen told him they had almost mistaken him for a Japanese paratrooper. Fuchikami insisted on delivering his messages, and kept going. He talked his way through a police roadblock with his identification and message to be delivered, then was waved straight into Fort Shafter without being stopped by the sentry. He delivered the message at about 11:45 and went home.

The message wended its weary, useless way through the confusion and arrived on the desk of the decoder. At about 3 P.M. it reached the desk of the section chief, who recognized its former value.

It was given to Lieutenant Colonel Carroll A. "Cappy" Powell. He treated it like a snake in a picnic basket, and called in his friend, Major Robert J. Fleming, one of General Short's most trusted aides and his personal troubleshooter. Powell, a veteran of several run-ins with the short-fused general, pleaded with Fleming to take the message to the general. He wanted to avoid this excellent opportunity to be the messenger who gets shot.

Fleming understood, and took the message to Short. Short accepted it and asked Fleming what he was doing delivering messages. Fleming told him that Powell did not want to be there because he knew Short would be extremely angry when he read it. Fleming was right; Short exploded.

Over at Pearl Harbor, Admiral Kimmel's reaction was the same when his copy finally arrived. He flung the piece of damning history into a wastebasket.

Even had the message arrived in time, one must wonder what effect such a vague message would have had on the general and the admiral. It fell far short of being a direct order to prepare for an attack or invasion, and the Hawaiian military had already missed several opportunities to prepare for the attack.

16

The White House Prepares for War

When Roosevelt called Cordell Hull and told him that Frank Knox had just called with news of "an air raid over Pearl Harbor," Hull swore but said nothing to anyone on his staff. Instead, he began rehearsing a brief speech for the Japanese envoys when they were permitted to see him. When Roosevelt's call came, Hull had two of his aides with him, Green Hackworth and Joseph W. Ballantine; they had been discussing what Hull should tell the Japanese. Then Roosevelt's call came, and Hull had to abandon his prepared statement.

Hull's first reaction was to send the envoys away without seeing them, but he decided against that. He had a few things to say to them. He called them into his office that a writer characterized as "impersonal as a railway-station waiting room." Hull had grown fond of Nomura, who had been a guest in his apartment several times. Not given to endearments, he showed his affection for Nomura by referring to him as "the old codger," a Tennessee way of saying "nice guy." On the other hand, he had never liked Kurusu and had referred to him as "that other citizen." And probably worse. He was well known among cabinet members for his outspokenness; for the past five or six years he had referred to the Rome-Berlin-Tokyo group as "gangster nations."

When the two Japanese were seated, Nomura apologized for their tardiness and said that while their instructions were to present the note from the government at one o'clock, the decoding had taken longer than they expected. Hull asked them why one o'clock was chosen, and Nomura said he did not know. Kurusu remained silent.

Nomura handed the note to Hull. The next ten or fifteen minutes have entered American folklore, and we can not be absolutely certain of the sequence of events that led up to Hull's brief lecture and dismissal. The most popular version is that when he was handed the 2,500-word document, he sat down, carefully placed his pince-nez on his nose, and pretended to read the document, which he had already been able to study at some length thanks to America's breaking the Japanese code. He used the ten minutes of silence to make the ambassadors squirm, if possible, and to compose his speech. Anger was not hard to manufacture because the events of the last hour had really set off a firecracker in the tough old Kentuckian's psyche.

At last he looked up. "I must say that in all my conversations with you during the last nine months, I have never uttered one word of untruth," Hull told them. "This is borne out absolutely by the record. In all my fifty years of public service I have never seen a document that was more crowded with infamous falsehoods and distortions; infamous falsehoods and distortions on a scale so huge that I never imagined until today that any government on this planet was capable of uttering them."

The Japanese were stunned. Nomura, who was fond of Hull and did not know why he was so angry, started to say something, but Hull cut him off. He wished them a good day and pointed to the door. They left without speaking, Kurusu impassive and Nomura looking hurt. With news of the attack common knowledge by now, reporters had been told of the meeting in Hull's office, and several were gathered outside the door when the Japanese emerged. They hurried away without answering any questions.

Both Japanese and their staffs remained in Washington as virtual prisoners until a diplomatic exchange could be arranged. They arrived in Yokohama in August 1942, with bad news for their superiors about America's unification and resolve.

Hull immediately sat down and dictated to M. J. McDermott, chief of the Division of Current Information, what he had told the diplomats so it would be recorded while still absolutely fresh in his memory. While he was doing so, President Roosevelt called. He asked how it had gone, and Hull told him the whole story. The President interrupted him occasionally with praise. "That's grand, Cordell," Roosevelt said at the end of Hull's story, obviously delighted that Hull had launched the first attack against Japan in such a dignified and eloquent manner.

Roosevelt then called in Henry L. Stimson, Secretary of War; General George C. Marshall, Jr., Chief of Staff; Sumner Welles, Under Secretary of State; and the British ambassador to the United States, Viscount Halifax, was called in so that our closest allies, the British, would be the first to know America was going to war.

However, transatlantic telephone service was so limited in 1941 that Halifax's call was not placed until about three o'clock that afternoon, 9 P.M. in England. It made little difference, because by that time the news had been spread throughout the world by radio.

When Roosevelt called Churchill at his country place, Churchill had already heard the news on BBC Radio and was, of course, delighted that America was in the war. He told Roosevelt he would keep his long-standing promise of declaring war on Japan "within the hour" after America had done so.

The war was not an hour old for the White House when President Roosevelt issued the first status report. He called his press secretary, Stephen Early, at his home. Early was still in his pajamas and dressing gown, engrossed in the Sunday papers.

"Have you got a pencil handy, Steve?" the President asked.

"Do I need it?" Early asked, expecting some kind of joke from the President.

"Yes," replied a serious President. "I have a pretty important statement here, and it ought to go out verbatim."

Early did not have a pencil in reach, so he asked his wife, who had been a stenographer, to take down the President's statement as he repeated the words to her.

"At 7:55 A.M., Hawaiian time, the Japanese bombed Pearl Harbor. The attacks are continuing."

Early looked at his watch; it was 2:22. He called for a White House limousine and scrambled into street clothes. As soon as he was dressed, he hurried his wife into the family Pontiac and proceeded to scare the daylights out of her as he hit sixty miles an hour and more heading down Sixteenth Street. He watched the traffic and told her to watch for the limo, which they met about halfway to the White House. He flagged down the limo and left his shaken wife to drive home.

At 2:35 P.M. the White House's switchboard superintendent, Louise Hackmeister, set up a conference call between Early and the three press associations: the Associated Press, United Press, and International News Service. Once all three were on, Early read them the prepared announcement, and "flash" bells on the ticker-tape machines all over America began ringing.

Those who spent that afternoon and evening with President Roosevelt later remarked on how calm he was throughout the day, and how brilliantly he conducted the first hours of the war. He spoke with Hawaii's territorial governor, Joseph B. Poindexter. He talked to Winston Churchill and the British ambassador to set into motion the declarations of war that he would deliver to Congress the following morning. He began writing the speech to be delivered to Congress with the request for a war declaration: "Yesterday, December 7, 1941, a date which will live in infamy, . . ."

The day wore on. More and more reports came in, none brighter than the last. The Japanese attacked the American bases in the Philippines. Japanese submarines sank a lumber ship between California and Hawaii. The Japanese attacked Hong Kong, Guam, Wake Island, and Midway. Reports of death and damage quickly became ordinary. A beautiful day that began in the Oval Office with a casual conversation between two close friends ended as one of the most grim days in American history.

17

War Becomes a Reality

On the afternoon of December 7, North Dakota Senator Gerald P. Nye, one of the most vocal members of America First, was scheduled to speak in the Soldiers' and Sailors' Memorial Hall in Pittsburgh. The hall was filled to its capacity of 2,500.

Robert Nagy of the *Pittsburgh Post Gazette* went to cover the speech and took along copies of the wire service stories about the attacks at Pearl Harbor and Manila. He was in for an interesting afternoon because Senator Nye loved to attack President Roosevelt's lend-lease program and the steady buildup of America's arsenal; he did not like to hear anything that might change his mind.

The meeting was scheduled to start at 3 P.M., just about the time the second and final wave of Japanese planes was breaking off the attack and leaving Pearl Harbor for their carriers. Nobody in the auditorium knew of the attack. Nagy found Senator Nye in a tiny room backstage with two other speakers, Irene Castle McLaughlin, widow of Vernon Castle, the famous dancer who was killed in World War I, and the Pittsburgh America First chairman, John B. Gordon.

When Nye read the news reports Nagy handed him, his first comment became one of a dozen or so uttered that day which will probably live forever: "It sounds terribly fishy to me."

Nye did not want to believe what he was reading, and probably felt as though part of the reason for his existence was being taken away from him. He turned to Nagy almost pleadingly: "Can't we have some details? Is it sabotage or is it an open attack?" Then he directed his anger where it had served him so well in the past: "I'm amazed that the President would announce an attack without giving details."

The meeting went on as planned, and since nobody in the audience knew of the attack, Nye and Gordon had a grand time denouncing President Roosevelt. Nothing was said about the attack, even though Irene Castle McLaughlin broke down when talking about losing loved ones and how devastated she was when Vernon was killed.

In the midst of the raucous cheering, a man stood up in the rear of the auditorium and began shouting that the meeting should be canceled. He was Enrique Urrutia, Jr., chief of the Second Military Area of the Organized Reserve. He had spent thirty-one years in the Army, and at that moment he was furious.

"Do you know that Japan has attacked Manila and Hawaii?" he shouted, unable to believe the America Firsters would be ranting if they knew. He was hustled out of the auditorium by police for his own protection. Nagy followed this procession into the foyer, and Urrutia told Nagy that he had attended because he thought it was a patriots' meeting.

"This is a traitors' meeting," he snapped as he was hustled away.

Nye spoke for an hour, during which time he said nothing about the Japanese attacks. Nagy was called to the telephone for an update on the attack and was told that the Japanese government had declared war on America and Great Britain. Nagy printed the information on a piece of paper, walked onstage and put it on Senator Nye's rostrum. Nye read it silently, said nothing about it, and continued his attack on Roosevelt for another fifteen minutes.

Finally, he seemed to tire of calling Roosevelt names and acknowledged Nagy's message. He read the note aloud slowly, then resumed his attack on Roosevelt, insinuating that America must have provoked Japan to make this happen.

Other members of the isolationist community were quicker to come around to the mood of mainstream America. Lansing Hoyt, chairman of the America First chapter in Wisconsin, told a reporter that "we should bomb Japanese cities to the ground," and that "America First had always been for defense. Now we are for offense. It looks like war with the Axis."

In Cleveland the Institute of Pacific Relations was meeting that afternoon with about eighty delegates in attendance, including congressmen, industrialists, and journalists. They were gathered to seek a solution to the Japanese problem in the Pacific. When the news was announced, everything that had been said earlier became obsolete. As one delegate said, "Japan has handed America its long-needed unity on a silver platter."

One of the journalists, James R. Young, had been stationed in Tokyo until recently. He told the group that four days earlier he had received a package from the Japanese consul in New York containing a file the Japanese government had been keeping on him before he was arrested in Tokyo and expelled. Young said he suspected they were cleaning out their desks.

Hugh Byas, another former Tokyo correspondent, reminded the group that in 1904 the Japanese had attacked Port Arthur in the same manner, including sending their ambassador to the Russian court ball at the moment the attack was being launched.

One young editor-writer, John R. Whiting, felt a sense of déjà vu that afternoon. He was home in Hastings-on-Hudson, New York, entertaining a German-born photographer named Eric Schaal, a refugee from the Nazis who did not yet have his American citizenship. Whiting's boss called and told him to turn on the radio, then said rather cryptically, "You're a hero. We've won the war."

Then Whiting had an opportunity to think back on one of the most popular articles he had ever written. He was associate editor of a pictorial magazine called *Click* that was published by the *Philadelphia Enquirer*. He was also a Navy buff, and almost exactly a year earlier he was doodling with some ideas and came up with a "what-if" idea: What would happen if Japan invaded America?

He showed it to his boss, and was given the go-ahead to write it and to work with an artist. Whiting told his readers that the story was imaginary, but urged them to remember what was not imaginary: that Japan had an alliance with Germany and Italy; that it had 9 battleships, 47 cruisers, 3,000 warplanes, and an undisclosed number of aircraft carriers; that Japan also had 59 submarines; and that it needed Mexico's oil.

With this grim prologue, Whiting's scenario had Japanese soldiers sneaking ashore in San Francisco from innocent-looking freighters. Then they headed south to conquer Los Angeles, where they herded eighty thousand civilian prisoners into concentration camps. The Japanese neutralized the Panama Canal by sinking a freighter at the Gatun Lock. Then they attacked Pearl Harbor and Manila. Whiting stepped into a bit of fantasy by saying that it was then learned that the Japanese bombers were launched from a "secretly built fleet of 10 submarine aircraft carriers."

As Whiting's war went into the third month, "Women's clubs, jellyfish Congressmen and a woman radio commentator argued fiercely that any peace was better than having homes burned, women and children beaten in concentration camps, and three million men forced to go into the army."

One of the first groups Whiting had fighting effectively against the Japanese was the prisoners of Alcatraz, whom the invaders freed so they could spread terror in America. Whiting knew what superpatriots prisoners tend to be, so instead of joining the invaders, they immediately turned on the Japanese and killed many of them while Naval Reservists blew up a Japanese cruiser.

The tide of Whiting's war turned as radio-controlled bombers and torpedo bombers took on the Japanese fleet. The Japanese then resorted to poison gas, but it was not enough. America was on the attack, and finally Admiral Yoshida surrendered to Admiral Richardson on the deck of the battleship *Washington.*

"From China to Alaska, from the Canal Zone to Seattle, from San Diego to Bangor, great bonfires are built for democracy," he concluded.

Whiting's tour de force brought an enthusiastic response from the military. He was invited to Washington, D.C., by one of his contacts in the Navy, wined and dined and praised. He was introduced to General Mark Clark ("He'll be one of the top generals," he was told).

Soon after the news came to Washington, D.C., crowds began gathering around the White House. One rather ominous group was in front of the Japanese Embassy on Massachusetts Avenue. The crowd remained quiet and polite, but police were called and officers were posted around the embassy. Some in the crowd were watching for the telltale plume of smoke from burning documents that signals the end of diplomatic relations with the host country.

They were not disappointed. Two embassy employees carried out papers, over which they poured a liquid, presumably gasoline, and lit them. In seconds the fire had consumed the papers and was out.

A reporter called the embassy and asked if they were going to request police protection. The spokesman said they were not, because they had faith in the fairness of the American people.

In the early evening the police superintendent went to the embassy gate but was refused admittance. He went to the kitchen entrance and asked how many policemen the embassy would like to have for protection. Apparently there was no reply, for he got into his squad car and drove away.

Similar incidents occurred at Japanese consulates all over the country. In Seattle police posted a guard at the home of Consul Yuki Sato and would not let anyone enter. However, when a group of children came to the gate to give a Christmas present to one of the Sato children, Gordon Lewis, the eight-year-old son of a Navy lieutenant commander, talked his way in and gave his friend, Syuki Sato, a toy automobile and dive bomber.

The elder Sato declined to make a comment to reporters who gathered at his residence, but James Y. Sakomoto, American-born publisher of a local Japanese-language newspaper, was outspoken: "Japan asked for it, and Japan will get it—in the neck."

Back in Washington, Hazel Amberg Holman, the daughter of Julius H. Amberg, special assistant to the Secretary of War, was a high-school student. She turned the radio on after the family finished Sunday dinner, and she was the first in the house to hear the news. "I must have been alone by the radio, because I remember rushing off to tell my parents, who hurried to the radio to confirm with their own ears what I was hearing," she said.

"My father quickly called his friend and colleague Robert Patterson, then Under Secretary of War. I'm not sure if he already knew of the events, but in later years we often joked that I was the one who alerted the top brass at the War Department of the situation.

"My father left for his office after making the call, and when he returned several hours later, he reported that troops had arrived and set up machine guns around the War Department. This activity was reported with some humor, since invasion did not seem imminent.

"My brother was home for the weekend on a pass from his base in Virginia—he had been drafted a few months earlier after his number came up in the second Selective Service lottery drawing. When we drove him to Union Station, we decided to take a tour of D.C. to see what was going on. We tried to drive by the White House, but as I remember, Pennsylvania Avenue had been hastily blocked off. We also drove along Massachusetts Avenue, since the word was that the Japanese were burning papers. As we drove by the Japanese Embassy, we tried to see smoke in the rear but all appeared disappointingly as usual.

"There were quite a few men in uniform at the station, like my brother, who were being sent off by their families. The farewells seemed unusually heartfelt and long, as if everyone was expecting all soldiers to be whisked off to war instantly."

Edward Stuntz was an Associated Press reporter covering Latin America. He rushed to the office when he heard the news on the radio, and began calling Latin American embassies for comments and information about other countries' reactions.

"We got a message that Costa Rica had declared war and had rounded up all the Japanese farmers in the country.

"My dear old friend Alvareo Concheso, the Cuban ambassador who was working for Batista, was furious. 'Mr. Stuntz, why is it that the Associated Press lets Costa Rica declare war before we do, the Cubans?'

" 'But Mr. Ambassador, AP didn't have anything to do with it. We just got a story, which you have read, that the President of Costa Rica announced that a state of war with Japan existed so that he could go out and arrest all these Japanese who might be subversives.'

" 'What am I going to tell Colonel Batista?'

" 'Tell him that Mr. Roosevelt is said to be preparing a message for Congress tomorrow,' I said.

" 'But you let Costa Rica declare war. Don't you know that Cuba is always the first to declare war after the United States?' "

A fourteen-year-old Boy Scout, Robert Knudson, was on his way home from an outing with his troop. Nobody had heard of the bombing as they drove through Green Valley, an area south of Seattle where many Japanese-American farmers lived. He remembers seeing many of the farmers gathered outside on their porches, talking, but did not think about it until much later.

Not all Americans were impressed with the news. Some remembered being taken in by Orson Welles's famous 1938 radio broadcast of an imaginary invasion from Mars. On the evening of December 7, many people across America were panic-stricken and began running about in the streets, jamming the telephone system, and sending police into a rage. Thus, when a New Jersey reporter for a man-on-the-street radio show stopped a man out walking his dog and asked him what he thought of the Pearl Harbor attack, he got a surprising answer: "Ha! You're not going to catch me on another of your pranks."

For some people, the business at hand was more pressing than something happening thousands of miles away. Romance, for example. Jack Watson, secretary to an Iowa congressman, was living in the home of

C. W. "Runt" Bishop, an Illinois congressman, and was a good friend of the congressman's son, Jack. Watson was at the office that afternoon talking on the phone to his girlfriend when the Capitol operator broke in and told him he had an urgent call.

"I heard the excited voice of Jack Bishop. He told me something was going on, and his father wanted me to find out what." The tone of voice—it was almost a command—irritated Watson. He snapped at his friend that he was talking to his girlfriend and would call back later.

The congressman's son wouldn't be put off. " 'Dad's at the Redskins game and says that for the last half hour the P.A. system has been instructing General This or Admiral That to report to their Pentagon offices. Dad wonders if that means an emergency has occurred. He is calling me back in ten minutes to find out what I've learned from you.' "

Watson was really irritated now. He reasoned that Congressman Bishop might be his landlord, but he was not his boss, and he resented taking orders from him. However, he agreed to call back when he did find out something, and in only a few moments he found out what the rest of America knew.

Tuck Lawlor's father was mayor of a small town in northern New Jersey. When the news came, everyone was in a different room of the house. Her mother, in the kitchen baking, was the first to hear it.

"We all heard Mom shriek: 'Hurry! Tom! Everyone!' We huddled around the kitchen table and heard the news. The telephone rang constantly, and then in midafternoon my brother, Richard, a year older than my twin sister and I, had an attack of appendicitis and was rushed to the hospital. While my mother sat in a dreary waiting room, my father drove my twin sister and me to a movie. We saw a double bill, *The Oxbow Incident* and *Wild Geese Calling.*

"Later, at home, all kinds of people kept coming to the house to confer with my mayor-father. He had to field questions like 'Where can we get sandbags?' 'Should I join the Army or the Navy?' Sheer panic."

In Oregon, Governor Charles A. Sprague was equally busy. After the announcement came, he went ahead with his schedule and visited the Oregon Shipbuilding Corporation on the Willamette River for a ceremony in which Mrs. Henry Kaiser was christening the USS *Thomas Jefferson* at 3 P.M. As soon as the ceremony was over, the governor went to the *Portland Oregonian* and sat down at a typewriter to compose a telegram to President Roosevelt. "We must not rest until menace of Japanese aggression in the Pacific is definitely ended," he wrote.

Then he proclaimed a state of emergency for Oregon, "precise meaning to be clarified Monday." This spurred the military people in the area into action. Guards were placed around Bonneville Dam, the Portland Water Bureau sent employees out to guard pipelines and reservoirs, and all bridges were placed under armed guard. All ships in port were frozen by the Navy. The ALCOA aluminum reduction plant across the Columbia River in Washington kept operating, but all yard lights were blacked out.

In Washington, D.C., all afternoon people walked slowly past the White House gates, some stopping to stand in a silent vigil, not expecting to see anything but taking comfort in knowing they were just outside the nation's nerve center. They still came in the darkness of evening. A silent traffic jam developed, with motorists having to wait through three or four light changes to drive a block. The people stood outside the iron fence around the White House grounds, watching the officials coming and going. Many stood on the steps of the old State Department Building for a better view.

Police were seldom seen and were unneeded because the crowd was so quiet and orderly. One policeman told a reporter that one reason so few of them were there was "Let four cops get together and four people come up. Let ten cops gather around and a hundred people come around."

Of all the government buildings open late that night, other than the White House, the only one lit up and filled with employees was the Munitions Building, where the Selective Service had its headquarters.

18

Extra! Extra!

In those pretelevision days newspapers were the primary source of news, and when something important happened—a war, a plane crash, a ship sinking, or a natural disaster—the competition among them was fierce. Today few cities support more than two newspapers, usually a morning and an evening paper, and often they share the same advertising and circulation staffs and are printed on the same presses. Only the news departments are totally separate.

The extra editions were therefore very important, and the newspapers raced to be the first on the street with them. All over America that Sunday afternoon these extras were being feverishly assembled in newsrooms by skeleton staffs. Most newspapermen hurried to the office as soon as they heard the news, much as military men rushed back to the base.

One of the proudest newspaper staffs was that of the *Chicago Sun Times,* which had just published its first issue on Thursday, December 4. The *Sun Times* hit the street at 7 P.M., beating the *Tribune,* the *Herald American,* and the other papers to the street by several minutes. Actually, the *Tribune* did not even print an extra edition; instead, it placed a banner, "Japan Attacks U.S.," across the top of its regular evening edition.

The Omaha *World Herald* got its extra edition on the street at about 4:45 P.M. and sold all 19,200 papers in a few minutes. The *St. Louis Globe Democrat* put out two extras, the second with an odd banner headline: MANILA QUIT. Some people may have considered it prophetic, but it was a typographical error. It should have read: MANILA QUIET.

The *Dallas Journal* and the *Dallas News* both went quickly to press. The *Journal* published three extras that day, the first appearing on the street at 3:50 P.M. and the last at 8:07; about 46,000 copies were sold, in addition to a copy free to every subscriber. The *News* did not appear until almost 6 P.M., and it sold 20,000 copies in less than an hour.

In Los Angeles, Bonnie Rockhill and her husband had been in town only a few days. That evening as they left a store near Fifth and Hill, they heard a paperboy shouting: "Read all about it! Japan just committed suicide!"

Newsboys set records for income that day. One was thirteen-year-old Cliff Goodall, who sold the *Reading Eagle* in Pennsylvania. "My first lesson in good business practice was learned that day," Goodall said. "We sold the three-cent paper for twenty-five cents and higher, whatever the market could handle. I made lots of money for a thirteen-year-old. But you know, I still feel bad about the excessive profits."

Reporters all over America were going through their telephone books, calling people for comments. One of the funniest was from the delighted Gung-hsing Wang, Chinese consul general in New Orleans. When the reporter called, an aide said Mr. Wang was "busy in the bathtub." Busy or not, he was anxious to talk to the reporters: "This will be the last time Japan has a chance to hit below the belly. As far as Japan is concerned, their goose is overheated."

Franklin W. Hooper, head copyboy at *Time* magazine, had arrived at the office at 8 A.M., his normal starting time. The magazine went to press on Monday night, so Sunday and Monday were the busiest days of the week for the editorial department.

"Shortly after 2 P.M. I walked by the teletype room and immediately felt that something was wrong," Hooper said. "It was the silence. There were six to eight machines in that tiny room, and always at least one of them was clattering away.

"The silence was eerie but didn't last long. Suddenly they all began chattering and clanging. The machines seemed peculiarly alive, as if they had something of the greatest importance to say, but were too nervous to say it.

"The Associated Press A wire kept clanging and printing FLASH over and over, but no message. I waited for what seemed an eternity. Since the AP had used the word FLASH only twice in its history, I felt compelled to stand by.

Eventually the message came: JAPS INVADE PEARL HARBOR—MORE KOMING.

"Since I didn't have the vaguest idea where Pearl Harbor was, I tore the copy off the machine and started running around the twenty-ninth floor of the old Time and Life Building, looking for a writer. Fortunately I ran into *Time*'s Far Eastern correspondent, Theodore White. He glanced at the copy. 'So the yellow bastards finally did it, eh?' he said."

19

Strange New Words

Looking back from the vantage point of half a century, many people say the event changed their lives for the better. One was Marjorie VanCott, a self-described "contented but slightly bored housewife—playing cards, Women's Club activities, and the usual civic activities.

"Along with thousands of other people, I was at Yankee Stadium watching the New York Giants playing; not too unusual. I don't remember which team won the game, what the weather was, only the brief announcement: 'Will General Donovan report to headquarters immediately.'

"It [the stadium] was quiet after that with just a steady undercurrent of concern, not excitement. We drove home by way of Bay Shore, having dinner at Cooper's Restaurant with a friend. My husband, who had been a quartermaster in the Navy in World War I, immediately talked of enlistment, and in less than six months was a lieutenant in the Coast Guard.

"When he was stationed in New York, I found an apartment for us, got a job in a bank, then followed him to San Francisco, working in an insurance company office. As soon as we got back home in 1946, I went into the insurance business, had my own agency for many years, and retired in 1987 after forty-five years of working, which I loved.

"All this was a result of Pearl Harbor."

However, for some people, the attack was almost insignificant. Initially it meant very little to people living in Okmulgee, Oklahoma, because on Saturday, December 6, a fire broke out in the local gasoline refinery and five of the big storage tanks exploded. Dorothy Strum had graduated from nursing school the previous spring and was working in the small hospital just a block from the refinery.

"I had signed up to join the Army Nurse Corps, which had been my dream," she said. "More than 300 people came through the hospital with burns and in shock. The city people gave sheets and linen for bandages, and medical supplies. It was a time of confusion and shock. Only five people died, and that was within the first hour. Others were treated for three months before they healed.

"The news of Pearl Harbor was alarming and far away, while our disaster was all around us and needed our attention. We would worry about Pearl Harbor later on, when there was time to think about it.

"Besides, it was my mother's birthday, and I had to call her and tell her about the explosion and that I was okay."

Joel I. Feinberg, seven years old, woke that morning with a very serious stomachache. After waiting a few hours for the pain to subside, his mother called her brother-in-law, who was chief of pediatric services at the Rhode Island Hospital. He came over, diagnosed it as acute appendicitis, and said Joel should be in surgery immediately.

"The hospital was very dark because all sorts of blackouts were in effect. Needless to say, this was a scary experience for a seven-year-old," Feinberg said.

Selma Stone had her appendix removed early that morning in Boston and was back in her room recovering when she heard the news on the radio.

"All our beds . . . were wheeled into the corridors, and there was a plan to move us out of the hospital. We all expected the waves of Japanese bombers to fly overhead and hit the city. When it was apparent that the bombers left Pearl harbor and didn't fly to San Francisco, I was wheeled back into my room.

"I often wonder where the hospital planned to take us, since there were no emergency routes [out of Boston]."

Other people in Boston were upset when the Civil Defense officials discovered that the city did not have an air-raid siren.

Ruth Hill Useem and her husband, John, were living in Vermillion, South Dakota, in 1941. He was teaching at the University of South Dakota and she was busy that weekend putting together a questionnaire on isolationism in the Great Plains. The questionnaire was to be part of an article a friend, Bert Loewenberg, was writing for *Harper's* magazine.

On that morning John was attending a fraternity gathering and she was typing the stencils for the questionnaire in their second-floor apartment.

"I had on a black quilted long bathrobe (the warmth in this northern-exposure apartment was not great), had on big, blue, fuzzy bedroom slippers (our ten-pound toy dog was lying there for warmth), and I had the New York Philharmonic on the radio.

"I was just on the second page of the stencils when the announcement came over the radio of the bombing of Pearl Harbor. As I recall, they continued with the concert afterward.

"But now I had a dilemma, especially after the declaration of war, for I had only the number of stencils I needed and some of the typed questions were now moot. We could not afford more stencils, so I remember having to use that blue correction fluid to blot out some questions and ask others.

"One of the questions which we then put in was 'How long do you think the war will last?'

"The usual answer was six weeks."

Children were not particularly impressed with the Pearl Harbor attack itself, but most detected a change in the atmosphere at home. For example, Marcia Jacobs Wollman remembers the day for a rather long Girl Scout hike she went on with her Newark, New Jersey, troop.

"Led by our two counselors . . . we took the 'tube,' the underground train, to New York City, then the subway to the Bronx [*sic*] so that we could walk back to New Jersey across the upper deck of the George Washington Bridge.

"It was a partly sunny day, but very cold and blustery. In those days girls wore short skirts, saddle shoes, and socks. Perhaps I had gloves and a kerchief. We each carried a bagged lunch.

"We proceeded to cross the windblown bridge on the sidewalk, single file, with cars whizzing by. Upon reaching the other side, we scrambled up the steep side of the New Jersey Palisades. By this time my fingers and toes were numb . . . when I stumbled and scraped my leg, I never felt it. Toward noon the day warmed a little, and we found a level area at the top where we ate our lunch.

"At about 6 P.M. we arrived back in Newark. Our parents met us at the Lackawanna railroad station, and everybody was excited and wanted to know if we had heard the news that Pearl Harbor was attacked.

" 'Who is she?' I wanted to know."

Don Rice of Mt. Vernon, Ohio, then a three-year-old, was playing on the living room floor when the news came.

"I had never seen adults in such an agitated state. Of course no one stopped to explain to me exactly what had happened.

"We had a family friend named Pearl Hay, and what I didn't understand was why everyone, even the radio announcer, should be so upset because some woman had exploded."

That day Grumman Aircraft on Long Island held an open house to show all the newest models, and five-year-old Sunni Eckhardt's father, a draftsman for the company, was not happy about it.

"My father was very upset because there were about eight Japanese businessmen crawling all over the fighter planes, taking photos," she said. "My Dad said that this was dangerous because we would shortly be at war with Japan.

"He was very tense and angry all day, even at the picnic. We drove my grandparents home to Yonkers. Grandpa turned on the radio, and the announcer was talking about the raid on Pearl Harbor. About two weeks later a neighbor boy who was a sailor came clicking down the sidewalk [he had taps on his shoes]. My mother said that this young man had survived the raid on Pearl Harbor. My Dad said, 'I know.'

"I always thought, as a child, that my Dad had the gift of precognition because of these incidents."

Robert McAfee, Jr., was four on December 6 but his parents decided to celebrate on the next day because it would be easier for all his friends to attend.

"We were living in Kensington, Maryland, and my father, a career Navy officer and graduate of the U.S. Naval Academy, was stationed in Washington, D.C.

"I remember sitting in a corner happily opening my presents when the phone rang. My father answered and cursed softly. He immediately went upstairs and put on his uniform. I remember my disappointment when my father abruptly left my party and didn't return until late that night. I saved some cake for him."

Edgar F. Dickson, Jr., then a nine-year-old West Virginia farm boy, was terrified by the attack because he was certain Pearl Harbor was up near Boston.

"I was sure the Japs would be down at the farm that very night," he said. "My mother got out an atlas and showed me where Pearl Harbor is, and I was satisfied the Japs wouldn't get me out of bed that night, anyway."

Wanda Gibson Richardson was ten years old. On December 7 she and her seven-year-old brother were going to meet their stepmother for the first time. On the way to his house, their father told them about the attack, but it meant nothing to either child.

"On our arrival at the house, the small radio was blaring out the same story," she said. "This strange fairy tale seemed to be true, but still I didn't know what all of the new words meant. It was scary.

"The next day my Daddy joined the Navy, and it was not long before I learned what the strange new words meant. Also, words like Seabees, Johnston Island, air mail, and censorship became familiar to me as the letters to my Dad and his lonely younger shipmates became a regular part of my young life."

Virginia Perkins Mason was twelve years old. Her close-knit family—mother, father, grandmother, aunt, and younger brother—were gathered in their home as they usually were on winter Sundays, playing mah-jongg and listening to the New York Philharmonic broadcast. When the broadcast was interrupted by news of the attack, her father jumped out of his chair and put his hands to his head.

" 'My God! There will be no more rubber shipments!'

"His textile factory depended on imported rubber, and in that split second I realized that our world had changed and would never be the same.

"My dad did, indeed, convert his mill to make bandoliers for the Army and nylon parachute cord. We were luckier than most, but it took a terrible toll on him."

Echoing what many people say about that day, she added, "Perhaps my experiences of that day are not too unusual, but it is a day which I shall never forget. The picture of that family scene around the living room fireplace is indelibly engraved in my memory."

It was the morning of Nestor Olavi Perala's confirmation in St. Paul's Episcopal Church in Bremerton, Washington. Since Bremerton was a major shipbuilding and Navy repair center, everyone there assumed it was as interesting a target for the Japanese as Pearl Harbor.

"As we came out of the church, an English chaplain who was stationed on a British battleship in the harbor came running to tell us that the radio news was reporting the bombing of Pearl Harbor.

"Everyone was glued to the radio all afternoon because we *knew* that if any place on the West Coast was going to be bombed, it would be Bremerton.

"There was no order from anywhere that a blackout would be in effect. It was so obvious that a blackout was urgent that everyone naturally observed it. We put blankets over the windows of every room that had to have lights on. People who needed to be driving at night drove without lights. I don't remember if anyone was killed, but I do remember several serious traffic accidents."

Eloise Paananen was skiing with a group of friends on Mount Rainier in Washington that day. Gradually news of the attack spread on the slopes.

"One of the kids was AWOL from the Army at Fort Lewis," she said. "We left early because [he] was supposed to report in. But when we got to Fort Lewis, the guards wouldn't accept our young man. We finally dumped him at the gate and got back in the slowly moving traffic to Seattle. We lost track of him after that."

Phyllis Dirks, who was eleven when the attack came, was the daughter of devout Mennonites who had left the Dust Bowl in North Dakota for the fertile soil of Idaho.

"The culture shock was horrendous," she remembers. "We had come from a one-room school in which nearly all the students were Mennonites. Here [in Idaho] the schools were consolidated and seemed enormous. In the one we attended first there were no others of our parents' faith at all. We were freaks to the other children and were treated, at best, with a grudging tolerance and at worst with open scorn.

"The Japanese attack on Pearl Harbor was announced grimly from the pulpit of our little country church at the evening service on December 7. No one at the time of morning worship had . . . possessed the news. We had, of course, no radios in our homes; they were strictly forbidden. How they heard the news at all, I have no idea; probably some neighbor told it.

"I remember the terror with which I faced the thought of school the next day. From what little our parents had said in our presence, we had come quickly to understand that now the world would be against us. We were afraid because our parents were afraid. It had not been clarified during the preceding major conflicts involving our nation how those opposed to combat of any sort would be dealt with by the government. Would the men have to go to prison? Would only young, unmarried men be called up and have to answer to their conscientious objection, or would those with families be expected to present themselves as well? No one knew."

The answers to these questions were presented to her immediately.

"At school our worst fears were realized, and we were treated as pariahs. Only a few children, mostly those outcast themselves for other reasons, dared the social risk of association with us. Even these few withheld some elements of true friendship in order to survive if it should become necessary to cut us loose and take their chances with the common herd.

"One girl was a special friend of mine. She was illegitimate, and for this crime against a decent society virtually the same pall of unacceptability hovered over her head as over mine. She had an older male cousin who had been good to her, and she was very attached to him. He joined the service right after Pearl Harbor and came to school in his uniform and spoke to us. Betty was almost literally bursting with pride.

"A few months later our bus dropped us off at the schoolyard, and I saw Betty in the center of a group over by the swings. I headed that way, and as I approached I could see that she was crying. She turned and saw me, and an expression of pure hatred crossed her face.

" 'Bob is dead,' she screamed at me, 'and it's your fault!' Then, surrounded by a group of children whose sympathy had for the moment overcome their social sensibilities, she turned her back on me and walked toward the schoolhouse. I couldn't speak, couldn't move.

"All through the years of the war, from the perspective of a child inside the Mennonite Church, I felt that we deserved the often angry shouts we heard when we made our infrequent trips to town for necessities. I felt we deserved to be treated as second-class citizens. I saw it as wrong to let others face mutilation or death to defend the right of us, and others like us, to take no part in any conflict.

"Now, though, from the perspective of most of a lifetime outside the church of my parents, I see that this is what America is all about: the right to hold firmly to an unpopular belief system and the right to have that system defended."

20

Sudden Heroes

For the men already in the military service, the attack meant, among other things, that the amount of time they agreed to serve when they enlisted no longer meant anything. Immediately an expression was invented: They were in "for the duration."

It also meant that the public changed its attitude toward servicemen for the better, and the change was instant. Men on their way back to their bases that afternoon and evening saw the changes, and some were not particularly impressed.

Julian Davidson was in the Air Corps at Mitchell Field on Long Island. That Sunday he was on a weekend pass in New York City. When he left the hotel that afternoon, he heard the paperboys hawking their extra editions, and almost immediately was stopped by a policeman, who told him all servicemen were to report back to their bases immediately.

"I went to Penn Station to take the Long Island Railroad to Hempstead, where an Army bus would take us to Mitchell Field. When I got to the Long Island Railroad, the conductor ushered . . . servicemen into the train and wouldn't accept fares.

"With a magical wand the doughboy was transferred from a despised human being into a hero! It was a known fact that soldiers from Mitchell Field were not welcome at Garden City, Long Island, a very wealthy community one stop before Hempstead and next to Mitchell Field.

"When the train stopped at Garden City, the conductors told us all soldiers were to get off at that stop and that the residents of Garden City, en masse, were at the station with their limos, cars, and chauffeurs and they would drive us directly to Mitchell Field."

Albert Schoenfield's experience was less dramatic but equally telling. He had been stationed at Mitchell Field for recruit training, then sent to Roosevelt Field, also on Long Island, a short distance away. He and a friend put on their civilian clothes and drove up to Hartford to visit girlfriends and to see the movie *Sergeant York*. As soon as news of the attack was flashed on the screen, they took the girls home and hurried back toward Long Island.

"At dinnertime we stopped at a Howard Johnson restaurant," Schoenfield said. "The wait would be an hour, we were told, so we told the hostess that although we were in civilian clothes, we had to return to the base immediately. In less than three minutes we were served.

"On our return to Roosevelt Field, it was now patrolled by bayonet-armed soldiers. In civilian clothes, and without any pass [none for weekends were required in peacetime], we were asked for the password. Of course we didn't know it, so we were held in detention for several hours until higher authority vouched that we were Air Corps personnel."

Most of the men who had gone AWOL seemed to stumble over their own feet getting back to their outfits. One soldier hiding out at home in Redding, California, turned himself in to the police that afternoon, telling them that he only wanted to get back to his company at Fort Lewis, Washington, and to his machine gun.

Bill Seril found out about the war in an unlikely situation.

"I was in Army basic training in Virginia, and unfortunately I had giggled during weekly barracks inspection that Saturday; the captain who was inspecting us had his . . . fly open as he austerely made the rounds of the barracks.

"Consequently, I was punished and assigned to latrine duty and confined to barracks for the weekend. So on Sunday, December 7, I had the rare distinction of learning about the Pearl Harbor attack while cleaning a toilet bowl."

Walter S. Hochner was a medical technician trainee stationed at Fort Eustis, Virginia. His best friend, Jack, was the company clerk, and on that Sunday he was on duty without relief. Hochner took lunch to him, and they sat and talked while Jack ate.

"He told me, in confidence, that a directive had been received that week giving the procedure for discharging draftees who had completed a year of service. He told me that after taking into consideration the induction date, age, and rank, he was seventh on the list and I was eighth.

" 'That's great!' I shouted.

"With that, the news came over the radio. Jack and I exchanged looks, he reached into the desk drawer, took out the list he had prepared, we nodded to each other without a word, and he slowly tore up the list."

War meant something else to a minister in Tacoma near Fort Lewis, Washington. Robert Ramsay had been drafted into the Army and was lucky enough to be stationed at Fort Lewis. He continued much of his normal life, including playing organ in the Episcopal Church of the Holy Communion.

On Pearl Harbor Sunday, the rector told the parishioners of the attack, and finished the announcement with "Well, there goes my organist."

Most military installations were in a state of confusion. Many of the officers in charge, seldom high-ranking officers because it was a weekend, tried to do what they thought was best. Many chose to assume the worst scenario and prepared the bases for attack.

Floyd Bennett Field in Brooklyn was a good example. Robert E. Machol, an ensign assigned to the naval air station at the field, was having lunch at his brother's house in Queens when they heard about the attack on the radio, followed by the order "All officers and men assigned to Floyd Bennett Field report immediately."

"I had the option of going back to Manhattan [where he lived] and changing into my uniform, but I decided the war would be greatly inhibited if I didn't get to Floyd Bennett Field as quickly as possible," Machol said. "So I took the crosstown subway directly to Brooklyn, then the bus out to Floyd Bennett Field.

"I was accustomed to getting off this bus every morning, walking through the gate without really giving much attention to the Marine guard, who always gave me a snappy salute which I returned equally snappy. On this occasion, being rather excited, I got off the bus and ran across the sidewalk to the gate. Apparently there was a Marine on guard who had never seen me before. I was in civilian clothes, and I came to a skidding halt with the point of a bayonet in my belly and a large Marine on the other end glaring at me and saying, 'You got any business here, son?'

"I raised both hands and told him I had ID in my pocket and asked if I could get it out.

"Inside, all was chaos. Someone had said the Grumman Aircraft factory a few miles away on Long Island at Bethpage had been bombed, and the assertion was generally accepted. We were all expecting to be next.

"Somebody gave the order to get all the airplanes out of the hangars. Most were little N2S and N3N two-seater biplanes used as trainers, and I can't imagine now why any enemy would have wanted to bother destroying them, but we rounded up all the enlisted personnel and had them push the airplanes out of the hangars.

"Half an hour later all the planes were indeed out of the hangars and scattered out to the farthest reaches of the field, when someone pointed out that they were all lined up on both sides of the runways because it was easier to push them down the runways, then over onto the grass. They were very vulnerable to a single plane going down the line and destroying them all with a machine gun, as had already happened at the fields in Hawaii and the Philippines. So the men had to go out again and move the planes around and scatter them all over the field.

"When they finally got back, they were all terribly cold and the first thing they wanted was a hot cup of coffee. But someone, in a moment of enthusiasm, had run all the civilians off the base, and the only people who knew how to operate the coffee machine and run the cafeteria were civilians. So we never got any coffee.

"Then somebody broke out the guns. I had never even known there were guns at the field, but there were thousands of them. Every man on the base got a rifle. I doubt if any of them had ever seen a rifle before, but we gave them rifles and live ammunition. It was a miracle that somebody wasn't killed.

"We anticipated a landing of troops from submarines, so we stationed men at about every twenty feet around the periphery of the base. Then I was told to go out along the periphery and see that everyone was at his assigned position and had a fully loaded gun. Most of the men knew me, and even though I was in civilian clothes, the first man I passed threw me a salute. Of course I had to salute back. Then the second guy threw me a salute, then the next, and pretty soon they all caught on, and as I walked along the periphery for the next twenty minutes, my arm got tired returning salutes."

In the middle of this confusion and danger of being shot by American soldiers on American soil, Machol received a phone call from his college roommate, Robert L. Zimmerman. As he often did, he spoke in his best German accent: "Zis is Tsimmermann. Vere are zose plans? Vot do you zink ve are payink you for?"

Machol was panic-stricken and said exactly the wrong thing: "For heaven's sake, don't do that over the telephone. Somebody might be listening."

Not all men got back to their bases immediately. Helen Cobb and her new husband, Marvin, then a Marine private first class, were visiting her parents while her father helped repair the couple's old car. She heard the announcement of the attack on the radio and ran outside to tell her husband and father. Her husband told her to listen to see if troops were being called in.

"As I entered the house, I heard all men in the Eleventh Naval District ordered to their stations. I waited for a mention of the Marine Corps. I knew little about the Corps, except that if Marines were supposed to have wives, they would have been issued with the seabags.

"Marvin went in the next morning at his usual time. I'm not really clear about all that happened, but I gather he stood at attention for some time before his commanding officer, trying to explain that his wife didn't know the Marines were a part of the Eleventh Naval District."

Walter Trenerry, a private in a Quartermaster Corps training unit in Cheyenne, Wyoming, was writing a letter to his parents in Duluth while watching a bridge game and occasionally listening to the New York Philharmonic playing Shostakovich's First Symphony. Nobody paid much attention to the first interruption, but then they heard the announcer say, "We repeat, the Japanese have attacked Pearl Harbor!"

"After the first shock I felt a sense of relief," Trenerry said. "The suspense was over. At last all this nonsense of saluting, Yessirring, twenty-five-mile marches, close-order drill, and the rifle range made some sense. Purpose replaced pointlessness.

"Under the Selective Service Act of 1940, we drafted men would serve one year on active duty and then go home, subject to recall as reserves. In the fall of 1941 the officers trying to induce us to enlist for three-year hitches had hard going. The general sentiments were 'America First.' 'Why fight for the damned Jews?' 'Let that sonofabitch Roosevelt fight his own war.'

"The training films were hopeless. The 'enemy' always wore some dreamed-up uniform never seen on earth and spoke a clickety-clackety foreign tongue that turned out to be Esperanto."

Trenerry finished his letter and mailed it, then went back to the barracks, where his sixty-three fellow draftees were talking about what the war would mean to them. One suggested that they all get together when the war was over.

"The sergeant, who always spoke of his earlier Army days as 'before I joined the Boy Scouts,' told us we could get together 'if you come back. I was with the bunch that went to Mexico in 1916. We thought it would be a lark, but when that was over, six faces in my platoon were missing.'

"At dinner the company commander announced that all furloughs, including the Christmas furloughs chosen two weeks earlier by lot, were canceled; that all civilian clothes, which we had been allowed to have in camp and to wear in town, must go; and that the guards would now be issued live ammunition and would fire on anyone who failed to stop when challenged.

"Later that evening I had a tearful telephone talk with my fiancée at Radcliffe, who never tired of insisting that I, a lowly private, should get busy pulling wires to get myself assigned to New York or Massachusetts."

In San Francisco John W. Quinlan, a young longshoreman, was out on the beach with a young nurse that afternoon and witnessed a comforting spectacle.

"At about 3:30 P.M., as we were walking along the beach, a newsboy came running down the beach shouting, 'War! Pearl Harbor has been bombed!' At that time I had never heard of Pearl Harbor, as I was only nineteen and my geography studies in high school left much to be desired.

"I bought a paper from the newsboy, and we sat on a beachfront bench and read the account of the bombing, then we continued on down the beach. As we got near the channel from the bay into the ocean, we saw Navy destroyers and cruisers heading down the channel into the open sea. They were going full speed, smoke coming out of the funnels, sailors could be seen on the decks, flags flying. It gave us a great uplift to see that the Navy was on its toes and going out to give battle. There must have been ten or more Navy ships that steamed out of the harbor going west.

"I told my date, 'The Japs are going to get it now—look at those ships go!' "

North of San Francisco, in the northern forest town of Yreka, a group decided to disband itself "for the duration." This was the State of Jefferson, a new state being carved out of northern California and southern Oregon by a group led by Judge John J. Childs of Crescent City, the governor of the forty-ninth state-to-be.

The organization, described in the California newspapers as a seriocomic group, at first considered declaring war on Japan on their own. But this idea was discarded in favor of making one last policy statement to accompany their disappearance. "In view of the national emergency," the statement said, "the acting officials of the provisional territory of Jefferson here and now discontinue any and all activities. The action we have taken was taken with the sole purpose of calling the attention of the proper authorities of Oregon and California and the federal authorities in Washington to the fact that we have immense deposits of strategic and necessary defense minerals, and that we need roads to develop these minerals."

After swearing total loyalty to the state and federal officials in defense of the country, J. P. Maginnis, executive secretary of the Jefferson Territorial Committee, signed the statement.

One place in America where the news was late in arriving was Palm Springs, which then seldom received radio programs during the day because of interference from the mountains that loom over it on the west side of town. Perhaps the first report came from a Navy officer there for the weekend who was recalled to his base by telephone. The story spread around the hotels, and when darkness brought better radio reception, the desert spa was in a more somber mood.

One of the girls was not impressed: "Everybody knew this was going to happen, so why spoil a perfectly good Sunday afternoon worrying about it?" And later: "They couldn't have bombed Pearl Harbor. That admiral I met in Coronado is in charge, and he is a perfectly lovely person."

21

The Mating Dance Continues

Many people remember December 7, 1941, for reasons in addition to the attack. It was a day of first dates, of weddings, of honeymoons beginning, of births, illnesses, and thoughts of death.

Catherine Henderson was on her first date with "the man I've been married to for forty-seven years and I met on December 6, 1941. We had our first date the next day. I lived in Breckenridge, Texas, and he was in the 45th Division at Abilene, which is about fifty or sixty miles from Breckenridge.

"We were in the car taking a drive over to Ranger, Texas, . . . and we heard the news on the car radio. I didn't think much about it until I got home that night. My only brother was in Manila, and my mother was really upset after she heard it on the radio. He never came back."

Barbara and Orville Olson were married in Seattle on December 6, 1941, and drove to Portland, Oregon, for their honeymoon.

"We were in the elevator going down to breakfast when we heard the news of the war," she said. "It was quite a shock. We immediately returned to Seattle."

Ilene Katz remembers the day more for what happened with her aunt and uncle than for the war itself.

"My aunt, Anne Book, was *very* pregnant. They lived in Paterson, New Jersey, and that evening she went to the movies with Uncle Milton . . . and she was very nervous about giving birth in the theater, as she said.

"During intermission the lobby was complete chaos, and my uncle was more excited than my aunt. She kept on insisting she was okay, but he forgot to tell her what he had heard [about Pearl Harbor] and she didn't understand why he was so excited. All he said was 'Lets get out of here and go home—it's safer there.' She felt perfectly safe; nevertheless, good Jewish wife that she was, she followed him out of the theater, where she finally caught onto what had happened.

"December 7 was her due date, but she still claims the excitement that evening prevented completion of the 'job' that night. While listening to the news reports on the radio December 11, she finally came through with the real call, and my cousin Stephen was born.

"Aunt Anne has always told the story 'cockeyed,' and Stephen says two-thirds of his birthday cards were sent to him for December 7 because they thought he was born in the theater."

The threat of war meant a lot to Moneta Stewart of Seattle that weekend because she had a very important reason to worry. After eight years of marriage she and her husband had found out the previous Friday that after five years of trying to have children, she was finally pregnant. "I was scared. I kept thinking, after all these years and here we were vulnerable to whatever might happen.

"We were lucky, though. In August of 1942 I had my baby, an eight-pound, twelve-ounce boy."

Irene Miller and her husband, Al, were playing bridge with friends that Saturday evening at their home in Evanston, Illinois, when suddenly she blurted out, "I don't know about the rest of you, but I have to get to the hospital fast. Now! They say you'll always know when, even with your first child.

"Ellen Irene Miller was born at 3:10 A.M. on Sunday, December 7, 1941.

"My joy was soon tempered, as I went to the hospital in peace and woke up to war."

The same thing happened when Kendra Jane Brown was born.

"I was told by my parents that when my mother went into labor, there wasn't a war and when she woke up after giving birth to me, the first thing my father said to her was, 'Elsie, we're at war.' I guess I took second place to that, and I was . . . their first child."

But there have been compensations.

"All through my life everyone remembers my birthday, and of course how old I am. People often come up to me when December rolls around and remind me that I have a birthday coming up—as if I could ever forget.

"My birthday was usually noted on our local radio station when I was growing up. Stan Morgan was then the announcer, and although there would be other birthday greetings that day, he would always note that I was the Pearl Harbor Day birthday girl." Also, the local paper usually ran stories about her birthday parties.

One woman told about her soldier husband, who was in a military hospital with the mumps that morning. When news of the attack came, orderlies went through the hospital taking temperatures. If their temperatures were below 106° F, the soldiers were pulled out of bed and told to report for duty. Her husband's fever was too low, and he was sent to sweep the runway. As long as the temperature stayed under 106°, they stayed out of the hospital.

"After the war he fathered three healthy children, so no permanent damage was done," she said.

Olga Pottker, whose Navy officer husband, Ralph, had dashed back to the USS *Phoenix* before getting to enjoy his breakfast, was visiting her mother-in-law before going out for the afternoon with friends when they heard the announcement on the radio.

"I immediately went down to the newsroom [at the *Peoria Journal*] to watch the news coming in on the teletype. Nearly all the staff came in, but since we were a morning paper, we didn't put out a special edition.

"They insisted on taking a picture of me for the paper, and I looked like I had been dragged through a keyhole.

"The thing I remember most keenly about the whole event was how thoughtful my mother-in-law was. She comforted me rather than worrying about herself, and she had two sons, my husband, Ralph, in Pearl Harbor and another son in New Caledonia. I just couldn't get over her concern for me.

"And it was six weeks before I heard that Ralph was safe."

John Bladen, a foreman at Douglas Aircraft in Long Beach, California, was in Glendale with his mother, selecting burial plots in Forest Lawn Cemetery.

"My brother Bob was in the Army Medical Corps, and we wanted to get him a plot, too," Bladen said, never expecting him to need it because of war.

"It was a nice sunny day, and my mother was taking advantage of it, to my consternation, to cover a whole hillside [looking] for just the right spot for the best view.

" 'Why a best view?' I asked. 'Do you think you are going to be able to look out and enjoy it?' But she explained that she wanted anyone who came to visit to have a nice view.

"While in the selection process we heard that the Japanese had bombed Pearl Harbor.

"Oh, yes, the salesman who was showing us around was named Mr. Moses."

Bladen's mother ran a boardinghouse that was then full of Navy and Air Force men and had a Japanese-American houseboy. She staunchly defended him and convinced the boarders that he could have had nothing to do with it.

"Since they all liked him, it proved to be no problem," Bladen said. "However, he was eventually sent to a camp with the rest of the Japanese Americans in California."

All through the afternoon and into the evening most people clustered around radios, listening to the latest news. The radio reporters were doing their best with the information at hand, but some permitted their imaginations to go galloping out of control.

The well-known analyst Upton Close reported that after the first attack there were "a few parachute troops wandering around on the sand on the north end of Oahu Island. They will soon be pulled in the bag and we'll find out who sent them."

No parachute troops or any other troops landed during the attack. One can only assume someone saw a Japanese pilot parachuting to safety after his plane was hit. Only two or three did that.

Fulton Lewis, Jr., went much further with his commentary five hours after the attack: "The Japanese must know, as all the rest of the world knows, that Pearl Harbor is the one invincible, absolutely invulnerable base in the world. It's stronger even than Gibraltar itself, and as far as any attack or siege of it is concerned, there could have been no possible sane intention on the part of the Japanese to such an end."

News of the attack did not reach everyone that Sunday. My own family knew nothing about it until Monday. We lived on a farm that was twelve miles from Gainsville, Missouri, six miles from the nearest telephone, and two miles from the nearest electric light. My oldest brother, Neil, was a high-school student then.

"Our parents had saved enough money to buy an old Model A when I turned sixteen, and I was the only one in the family who knew how to drive it; our parents didn't learn to drive until sometime in the 1950s. They bought the Model A so I could go to high school; there weren't . . . any school buses that came near Howards Ridge. So every morning I picked up two other kids, who helped buy gas, and we drove down to the Norfork River, right on the Arkansas line, and parked the car on the west side. Then we rowed a boat across the river—this was just before Norfork Dam was built—and caught the school bus on the other side, which took us to high school in Bakersfield. It was pretty rough on our parents in the winter because we rowed across the river no matter the hour of day or the kind of weather, and there were a few times when it got pretty hairy.

"The Pearl Harbor attack was on Sunday, and sometime Monday afternoon at school somebody said something about Pearl Harbor being bombed: 'Let me see, where is that? Is that where they dive for pearls?' We had no idea at all. And we didn't have any idea how important it was to us."

22

The Nation Unifies

As darkness descended across America, the American resolve that Admiral Yamamoto so feared had already become a reality. Reporters witnessed a unification that had never been experienced before, and certainly has not been experienced since. It was instantaneous and it was complete. All uncertainty was gone. People everywhere were saying the same thing in various ways:

"Now we can be unified."

"They stabbed us in the back."

"Goodbye, Tokyo."

"There's been too much talk and not enough action. Let's get going."

"Let 'em have it. They asked for it."

"Those Japs must be crazy."

"Why, them sons of bitches."

Soon after the attack was announced by Steve Early from the White House, the military apparatus began taking control of many aspects of society. If it is true that the first victim in a war is truth, then censorship is the first victory. The military mind loves control and secrecy, so the first thing General Short did when he took command of the Hawaiian Islands was to establish a censorship policy.

The same thing happened in Washington, D.C. When the war was about five hours old, Brigadier General Alexander D. Surles, chief of the Army's Press Relations Section, called a press conference to announce the censorship rules. More than fifty reporters gathered in the Munitions Building that evening after struggling through police barricades and Army patrols; the Army had already outfitted its guards with gas masks, guns with live ammunition, fixed bayonets, and aggressive attitudes. Fortunately no shots were fired.

The general wasted no words. He told the reporters that their relations had been pleasant in the past, but now they had reached a new phase. "All irresponsibility must stop," he ordered, without specifying what he considered irresponsible.

"It has become necessary for the War Department to invoke the act of April 16, 1918. It is a somewhat detailed act but, as it concerns you immediately, I emphasize these points. You and your papers cannot print any references in any way to troop movements, disposition, location, designation, components, or strength outside of the continental U.S. No references can be printed to the movements of troop transports, even if they are in the waters of the continental U.S."

No responsible reporter would want to write about those things anyway, and they were understandably smarting from the general's opening salvo, so the first question was about his irresponsibility charge. The general was not specific in his answer but said, ominously, that "certain information" had been printed that must have given considerable comfort to potential enemies. His reply gave no comfort at all to the reporters, who were already expecting heavy-handed censorship in the name of national security.

The general added that he did not want the word "censorship" used because he disliked it and its implications. Instead, he preferred the much less threatening and digestible word "restrictions": "Restrictions are necessary and restrictions are what we are imposing tonight," he said. Only the most naive reporter would have seen the difference.

The Japanese embassy and consulates across America were focal points that night. The crowds that gathered outside them early in the day were still milling around as darkness fell. The riots that employees and local police feared did not happen.

The local police and the staff of the New Orleans consulate felt a bit uneasy when a crowd estimated at two thousand gathered outside at dusk. A squad of police arrived, some on foot and others on motorcycles, to control the crowd. Everyone watched quietly as the employees burned piles of paper in wire trash burners. A woman next door was greatly concerned, fearing the wind would blow burning bits of paper onto her house. When the fire threatened to get out of hand, the fire department was called; they doused the burners with water and took the charred papers with them to the station.

Eventually the crowd drifted away. By 11 P.M. only the police and newsmen were left. The consul, Kenzo Ito, brought out eight cans of beer and a thermos of tea for them.

The police were especially busy in San Francisco, which had the largest number of Orientals of any city in North America. So many people drove through the Japanese section to stare that the police soon had a giant traffic jam to clear away. Once that was accomplished, they closed the entire area to all traffic for the rest of the evening.

People who drove through the district before the closure told reporters that shades were drawn and most shops were closed. The Japanese-American citizens the police considered dangerous were taken into custody, but no street trouble developed.

San Francisco's mayor, Angelo J. Rossi, had other things on his mind besides the safety of Japanese-American citizens, and he seized on the opportunity to call a halt to the several labor disputes in progress by declaring a state of emergency and ordering all employee and employer groups to "terminate their existing differences." It was a tall order because sixteen strikes were in progress on that day.

The Golden Gate Bridge was darkened that night, for the first time since it was opened, and that, as much as anything else, made the day memorable for San Franciscans.

23

Hawaii's Longest Night

It was Hawaii's longest night. With the radio stations off the air and only the calm voice of Jimmy Wong, the police dispatcher, for information, rumors swept the islands. Darkness comes swiftly in the tropics, and with the entire island of Oahu blacked out, fear became an epidemic. Nobody knew anything, nothing could be seen moving on the streets, and few people with guns were trained in using them. It had been more than twenty years since any American serviceman had fired at an enemy, and many of those with rifles and sidearms were civilians trying to help.

Several times that night guns, from antiaircraft cannon to pistols, were fired at imaginary targets. In spite of the general confusion, the emergency agencies in Honolulu went about their business in a generally orderly fashion. The leaders and corps of volunteers stayed up most of the night, blacking out windows and building light traps over doorways. The Red Cross and Salvation Army kept their canteens going around the clock, and the latter stationed men in front of its headquarters, on both sides of the darkened street, to tell everyone passing by that food and drink were inside. By midnight they counted 127 meals served, many of them to men coming back to town from Pearl Harbor who had not eaten since breakfast.

Although petty crime and looting were not a problem in Honolulu, the police were very busy and frustrated. They banged up the patrol cars by bumping into things in the darkness, or being bumped into. If they ran out of gasoline, and several did, there was little or no hope of getting more until daylight. The officers had to trudge back to headquarters on foot.

An interesting sidelight to the attack and subsequent martial law, blackouts, and general panic was the great number of rumors that spread immediately. Some of them are still alive, and will probably live as part of Hawaii's folklore. Perhaps the most persistent is that the Japanese bombed Honolulu. They did not, and the Army said so immediately after the attack; the explosions were from American antiaircraft shells that did not detonate in the air because of faulty manufacturing or poorly trained troops firing them.

One of the best books about the raid and its impact on the islands, Gwenfread Allen's *Hawaii's War Years,* lists the dominant unfounded rumors that burst forth full grown that day and night.

That Japanese spies murdered a Navy officer who had stumbled into one of their meetings while on a hike sometime before the attack.

That the people of Japanese ancestry in Hawaii were warned in advance of the raid.

That Japanese maids had refused to go to work that morning.

That newspaper advertisements carried warnings and instructions to Japanese citizens. [This one was a classic, and worriers found more than two dozen "messages" in a single furniture advertisement that had been published many times over the years at Christmastime.]

That several Japanese clubs and organizations held open houses that Saturday night so they could get American military leaders drunk.

That General Short refused to get out of bed when he was told of the attack.

That Admiral Kimmel refused to leave a golf game when the attack occurred.

That arrows pointing to targets had been cut in the cane fields.

That Japanese drivers deliberately blocked traffic between Honolulu and Pearl Harbor that morning.

That people in a milk truck opened fire with machine guns against the men fighting at Hickam Field.

That Japanese plantation workers ambushed servicemen.

That Japanese paratroopers were landing.

That the Japanese carriers had been found south of Hawaii and sunk.

That some of the pilots shot down were former residents of Honolulu and were wearing local high school and University of Hawaii class rings.

That the water supply had been poisoned.

That ammunition had been found in the homes and businesses of Japanese Americans.

That cane fires were set as signals for the invaders.

That Japanese-American store owners sold only to other Japanese Americans.

There were many more, and an equal number sprang up on the military bases that long, frightening night: The men were told that San Francisco had been attacked, as had the Panama Canal; that the USS *Pennsylvania* had taken two Japanese aircraft carriers under tow (although the *Pennsylvania* was still in port badly damaged).

One sentry was so trigger-happy that everybody was afraid to go near enough to relieve him, and he stayed on guard all night.

An officer who had ordered his men not to smoke that night was almost shot by one of those men when he forgot and lit a cigarette.

Several American lives were lost that night because of this pervasive fear. One of the worst incidents was the plight of the six fighter pilots from the *Enterprise* who had been out searching for the Japanese fleet. They returned to the carrier when it was too dark to land and, without realizing the danger, the carrier told them to go to Oahu and land at Ford Island.

The word was passed as well as it could be for the defenders to hold their fire because the incoming aircraft were friendly. But somebody either did not hear or got nervous, because a BAR (Browning automatic rifle) opened fire when the planes came in to land, and it was followed by virtually every kind of gun on the ground.

One of the pilots dived at the shooters with his landing lights on to blind them, then turned tail and went to Barbers Point to land. One plane crashed into the Palm Inn at Pearl City. Another pilot bailed out of his plane but was riddled with bullets as he parachuted down. Another crashed at Wheeler and was killed. Another spun in on Ford Island and lived, and another bailed out and survived. The squadron leader, Lieutenant (j.g.) Fritz Hebel, had stayed in the air during the confusion; and when the shooting stopped, he called the control tower, again, for landing instructions. They told him to come in as fast and as low as he could, and without landing lights. He landed safely.

Out at sea the destroyers darted about nervously in search of the enemy that had already departed for Japan. The American warships searched all around the islands without finding any more submarines. Aboard the USS *Henley,* Don Wilson, the torpedoman who had accidentally set off the General Quarters alarm just minutes before the attack, was still in his white uniform. He alternated between the bridge, where he stood helm watches to steer the ship, and the fantail, where he worked on torpedoes and depth charges. He was to be on duty, without time to change out of his uniform or to sleep more than a few minutes, from 4 A.M. Sunday until Wednesday, when the captain noticed how seedy he had become and sent him to bed. Ironically, Wilson would go through the entire war and never fire a torpedo at an enemy vessel. However, he did have to sink two American vessels that were too damaged to save.

The fear of invasion in Hawaii would continue for several days. Several civilians were killed by frightened soldiers, including at least six fishermen who were shot and killed when they returned home without knowing that the military had announced in newspapers that all unidentified boats would be sunk.

The rumor that Japanese paratroopers had landed was given some added fuel by a severed communication line that everyone assumed, in the heat of the battle, had to be a result of sabotage. The truth is less thrilling to contemplate.

Paul A. Fraser was executive officer of a battery company stationed at Schofield Barracks. The unit's cannons were 1898 British 75s located at the mouth of Kaukonahua Gulch.

"Just after we left Schofield, one of the few planes that got off the ground was shot down," Fraser said. "He came in smoking and crashed in a pineapple field. We pulled his body from the plane and proceeded on to our position.

"As we were digging in the guns, one of the cannoneers saw a big root and took an axe to it. The root turned out to be the main communication cable from the north side of the island to Army headquarters at Fort Shafter.

"By now the radar station at Kahuku was back in operation and was communicating with Army headquarters through the cable we had just cut. The ax cut the cable completely. We sent a message back through our own network, but it was noon before the Signal Corps was able to find us and repair the damage.

"In view of everything else that had happened that day, the island headquarters had assumed it was a case of sabotage. The battery had never been shown the location of the cable, even though the area was clearly marked as a battery position."

Throughout Hawaii the silencing of the radio stations was a major factor in the epidemic of unfounded rumors, and military censorship required a closed-mouth approach to denying or confirming rumors: "If they don't deny it, then it must be true." With no comment from those in charge, the worst possible scenario becomes the easiest to believe.

The night was excruciating for the military wives and children as they waited in the stifling darkness to hear if their men were dead or alive, wounded or whole. Many women without children went to the hospitals and evacuation centers to help however they could, and some women with needed skills, especially in medicine, left their children with friends.

It would be several days before all men were accounted for and all families reunited. Funeral services were held for the dead, and the hospitals were filled to overflowing with the wounded. The generosity of the Hawaiian people created problems in the hospitals and evacuation centers because it seemed everyone on the island insisted on helping with any job that needed to be done.

One teenage girl was seen that evening moving from stretcher to stretcher, comforting the victims, many of whom were dying. She gently held horribly wounded men until they died, then moved on to the next. Many civilians suffered deep emotional reaction to the raid, and at least one committed suicide a few days later.

Everyone knew that evacuation of dependents back to the mainland was inevitable, and everyone dreaded it. Over the next few weeks ship after ship loaded with women, children, and belongings would make the frightening journey from Honolulu to San Francisco, Los Angeles, or San Diego. The passengers, terrified of Japanese submarine attacks, had to wear life jackets constantly. The Navy did not have enough ships to provide escorts, which made it even more frightening.

As people settled down to try and sleep that night, the Hawaii they had known that morning was gone forever. It was no longer a gentle paradise. Now it was a battleground. Of all the places changed by the war, none would be changed more drastically than Hawaii. It would become one of America's major military installations and America's crossroad in the Pacific. Like the country to which it belonged, events overtook and overwhelmed it.

24

Defending the East Coast

By day's end, recruiting offices were open all over America. The office in Norfolk, Virginia, remained open all night. In Seattle the Marine Corps recruiting officer was called at home because so many young men were already at the office, demanding to volunteer immediately: Between 6 and 9 P.M. that Sunday evening, eighty-one men enlisted. This was not an unusual occurrence. All offices across America told radio stations and newspapers that they were extending their hours, beginning Monday. Several recruiting officers asked their superiors to be transferred to combat duty.

John J. Slattery, the engineer working on radar research in New Jersey, was deeply concerned about the attack because he was certain the radar system that he had helped design and that was installed in Hawaii worked perfectly. He and other members of the developmental team at Fort Monmouth could not understand what had happened. They could not imagine why the operators had not warned headquarters that the Japanese planes were coming.

His research team had a station at Twin Lights on Atlantic Highlands, a rise about 150 feet high overlooking the approach to New York Harbor. Another station was built in Meriden, Connecticut, and they had used them together to test the newest equipment, the SCR-270, with Army Air Corps planes coming in from the Atlantic.

"The Air Corps had found the system acceptable," Slattery said. "At that time it meant the two sets agreed within a mile or so, close enough for fighter planes to intercept incoming enemy planes."

He had spent most of the day listening to the radio, talking to other research engineers, and fretting about what could have happened in Hawaii. They had no way of knowing how badly warnings had been handled there.

That evening his boss, Paul Watson, called in a state of high excitement. "For God's sake, get out to Twin Lights and get the SCR-270 on the air," he shouted. "There's a report that the Germans are going to raid New York tonight."

Watson also told Slattery that an Army communications crew was on the way to tie the Twin Lights station into the entire military warning network.

Slattery called another engineer, Wilbur Brown, who lived across the street from him in Shrewsbury, New Jersey, and they jumped into Slattery's car and roared out to Twin Lights. The route was along Rumson Road, then a narrow, crooked farm road. Slattery gave Brown the ride of his life, driving sixty to sixty-five miles an hour on the dark road.

"When we turned on the set, we were supposed to give it at least a minute to warm up the filament, but I told Wilbur to hell with it, turn it up full. Nothing blew."

Slattery and Brown were kept busy far into the night as the Army communications team arrived to tie them into the network and other members of the research team showed up. Later in the night they were told that it was a false alarm and they went home. The Germans and Japanese had not coordinated the attack after all.

"We still felt heartsick not knowing why the Hawaii radar system had, as we thought, failed. About twelve days later we heard the full, true story and were shown a copy of the plot of the actual raid. Then, to our enormous relief, we knew the SCR-270 had detected the raid but the data had been ignored."

Military bases on both coasts were in a state of panic because of rumors that the Japanese were going to invade the West Coast and the Germans the East Coast. Servicemen got their first taste of what life would be like for the next four years.

Edwin A. Weber was in the Army Air Corps and stationed at Pope Field, Fort Bragg, in a lighter-than-air unit which used balloons. He was home on leave in Annapolis and had gone to the Washington Redskins–

Philadelphia Eagles game at Griffith Stadium, where he heard about the attack.

With no orders to return to his base, he went to a hockey game that night at the Uline Ice Arena in Washington. It was there he heard the order for military personnel to return to their stations immediately.

"I drove to Annapolis and changed into uniform and returned to Washington, D.C., caught the Atlantic Coast Line to Fayetteville, North Carolina, and on arrival at Pope Field was confronted by hastily dug slit trenches and a state of confusion on the part of personnel who had remained at the station."

Charles W. Kay had just been promoted to temporary sergeant in the Coast Artillery at Fort Monroe, Virginia, and was visiting his father on the family farm near Fredericksburg, Virginia, when the attack occurred.

"I was waiting in the bus terminal in Fredericksburg for the return trip to Fort Monroe," he said. "We had no news at the farm, and people kept looking at me in a strange way. I checked my fly and other buttons, and was drifting off in a snooze when a newspaper headline caught my eye. Pearl Harbor!

"I reported in that evening, and no one was in the battery office. The fort was on full alert, expecting a Japanese fleet reportedly coming down from New York. All the twenty-inch guns were manned, and our antiaircraft battery had moved into the casemates, running practice alerts every hour on the hour, carrying the heavy director and rangefinder out of the casemates and up onto the parapet.

"I told my first sergeant this was all bullshit. The Japanese fleet wasn't going to risk being bottled up in Chesapeake Bay. The next morning I was sent with a detail to set up a .50-caliber machine gun on the beach to repel enemy landing barges. I concluded that the only reasonable spot was behind a seawall in the middle of a flower garden in front of a colonel's home. It afforded concealment, a field of fire, and an avenue of support. My mission was canceled."

Kay was able to join his brother's unit headed overseas and was promoted to sergeant. His new battery was made up of "guardhouse habitués," regular Army sergeants who had taken a demotion to get a ninety-day furlough, and draftees whose year of service was almost up. They went by train to San Francisco and were billeted in the basement of the Cow Palace. On Christmas Eve, Kay was asleep in his bunk, fully dressed and wrapped in every sheet he could find, when a major, a captain, and two military policemen woke him. The major asked where all his troops were. Kay looked around and found that he was the only one there. Everyone, officers included, had gone AWOL. It was not long before he gave up in disgust and went into Officers Candidate School.

Some events, like childbirth, do not respond to historical moments; they just happen at the same time. That was the case with Benjamin J. Goodman of Los Angeles, who had driven to see his mother that day, accompanied by his four-year-old son, Richard.

"We were on our way back between 10 and 11 A.M. when I heard loud sirens coming from vehicles going the same direction I was. I was in the center of Sunset Boulevard, giving a signal for a left turn onto Scotland Street, where we lived.

"I suddenly saw a whole caravan of military vehicles trying to pass me on the left, and I immediately pulled to the right and stopped to avoid a collision. I was upset and decided to get on the telephone and report it to the Army. When I got home, my wife, who was pregnant with our second child, met me outside, all excited, telling me what had just happened at Pearl Harbor. I then knew why the military trucks were in such a hurry.

"That afternoon I took my wife to the hospital, where she gave birth to our daughter the next morning, at the very time the U.S. Congress was in session declaring war on Japan.

"After leaving the hospital that Sunday night, which was in total darkness except for flashlights and candles, I found my way in darkness to my car. The entire city of Los Angeles was in darkness by order of the President. I could not drive home with the lights on, so I put the car in low gear, stood on the running board, steering the car, and got home that night after several hours."

25

"I Slept Like a Baby"

Neither Edward R. Murrow nor Eric Sevareid, the CBS radio commentators, was surprised by the day. They had seen too many similar events firsthand in Europe over the past two or three years. Sevareid had begun the day with a visit from Phil Potter, an editor on the *Baltimore Sun* who had been in school with Sevareid at the University of Minnesota. A neighbor rushed over, tapped on Sevareid's window, and told him to turn on the radio. He did so, then rushed off to the White House press room, where he was to give some of the most reasoned, accurate, and sensitive radio reports of that long, long day.

That evening Edward R. Murrow had been invited to join the Roosevelts and Hopkinses for dinner. Given the circumstances, Murrow called Mrs. Roosevelt and offered to cancel. She would not hear of it. "We have to eat anyway," she reasoned. So Murrow ate with them and late that night went back to the CBS office, where Sevareid was working on his last broadcast of the day. Murrow said that Roosevelt was especially upset over having American planes destroyed on the ground instead of in the air, and kept repeating his disbelief that the Japanese caught them on the ground both in Hawaii and in the Philippines.

"What did you think when you saw that crowd staring through the White House fence?" Murrow asked Sevareid.

"They reminded me of the crowds around the Quai d'Orsay a couple of years ago," Sevareid replied, remembering Paris when the Germans invaded France.

"That's what I was thinking," Murrow agreed, remembering the months he had spent covering the Battle of Britain. "The same look on their faces that they had in Downing Street."

Sevareid went back to his writing, and seven hours after the attack his familiar voice of calm and reason was heard over the din of the White House press room. His dispatches from Europe in a soft, unassuming, and unbroadcast-like voice had become familiar to millions of Americans. He and the more theatrical Murrow were perhaps the most trusted voices in radio at that time. Americans had sat transfixed while listening to their reports from various parts of Europe as the war ravaged America's mother countries.

"Out on Pennsylvania Avenue," Sevareid began, "you can see the policemen walking back and forth, and then across the street in the dim street light you can see from this porch a mass of faces all turned this way, a patient crowd standing there in the chill evening, simply watching this lighted portico of the White House as the figures come and go. And to me I must confess there is a very familiar look and feeling about this whole scene. I've seen it in similar moments in Downing Street, in the Quai d'Orsay in Paris . . . the same crowd as these watching, waiting faces of ordinary citizens. . . .

"Now there is one report which I must give you which is not at all confirmed—a report which is rather widely believed here and which has just come in. And that is that the destruction at Hawaii was indeed very heavy, more heavy than we really had anticipated. For this report says that two capital ships of ours have been sunk, that another capital ship has been badly damaged, and the same report from the same source says that the airfield hangars there in Hawaii were completely flattened out and that a great many planes have been damaged. There is no speculation about the number of planes. Now if the planes were dispersed on that airfield as they normally would have been, with piles of earth around each one, the number of planes damaged probably was not great. But if the field was overcrowded for a possible emergency, then no one knows how many have been lost.

"Now I repeat, this report has not been confirmed, but it has come in from a fairly reliable source and many reporters here indeed believe it."

After this, Sevareid called it a day and went home. He felt the way many Americans felt that night: At last the war had really begun. It was out in the open, and nobody doubted how it would end.

"For me there was a feeling of enormous relief, the feeling that we had won, even before the fight began," Sevareid wrote in his autobiography, *Not So Wild a Dream,* in 1946. "I slept like a baby."

Bibliography

BOOKS

Allen, Gwenfread. *Hawaii's War Years: 1941–1945.* Honolulu: University of Hawaii Press, 1950.

Bergamini, David. *Japan's Imperial Conspiracy: How Emperor Hirohito Led Japan into War Against the West.* New York: William Morrow, 1971.

Bowman, Nelle E., King, Allen Y., and Wilson, Howard E. *This Is America: Our Land, Our People, Our Faith, Our Defense.* New York: American Book Company, 1942.

Bradley, John H. *The Second World War: Asia and the Pacific.* Wayne, NJ: Avery Publishing Group, 1989.

Brereton, Lewis H. *The Brereton Diaries. March 10, 1941 to August 5, 1945.* New York: William Morrow, 1946.

Broadfoot, Barry. *Six War Years, 1939–1945.* Toronto and Garden City, NY: Doubleday, 1974.

Childs, Marquis W. *I Write from Washington.* New York: Harper & Brothers, 1943.

Daley, Robert. *An American Saga: Juan Trippe and His Pan Am Empire.* New York: Random House, 1980.

Davis, Forrest, and Lindley, Ernest K. *How War Came: An American White Paper from the Fall of France to Pearl Harbor.* New York: Simon and Schuster, 1942.

Dunning, John. *Tune in Yesteryear: The Ultimate Encyclopedia of Old-Time Radio, 1925–1976.* Englewood Cliffs, NJ: Prentice-Hall, 1976.

Fergusson, Bernard. *The Watery Maze.* London: Collins, 1961.

Hoopes, Roy. *Americans Remember: The Home Front.* New York: Hawthorn Books, 1977.

Ito, Kazuo. *Issei.* Seattle, WA: Japanese Community Center, 1973.

Leonard, Thomas M. *Day by Day: The Forties.* New York: Facts on File, 1977.

Lingeman, Richard L. *Don't You Know There's a War On?* New York: G. P. Putnam's Sons, 1970.

Lombard, Helen. *While They Fought.* New York: Charles Scribner's Sons, 1947.

Lord, Walter. *Day of Infamy.* New York: Henry Holt, 1957.

Phillips, Cabell. *The Forties: Decade of Triumph and Trouble.* New York: Macmillan, 1975.

Prange, Gordon W. *At Dawn We Slept.* New York: McGraw-Hill, 1981.

———. *Pearl Harbor: The Verdict of History.* New York: McGraw-Hill, 1986.

———. *December 7, 1941: The Day the Japanese Attacked Pearl Harbor.* New York: McGraw-Hill, 1988.

Satterfield, Archie. *The Home Front: An Oral History of the War Years in America, 1941–1945.* New York: Playboy Press, 1981.

Sevareid, Eric. *Not So Wild a Dream.* New York: Atheneum, 1946, 1976.

Sheehan, Ed. *Days of '41.* Honolulu: Pearl Harbor-Honolulu Branch 46 Fleet Reserve Association Enterprises, 1976.

Sherwood, Robert. *Roosevelt and Hopkins: An Intimate History.* New York: Harper, 1948.

Time, Inc. *December 7: The First Thirty Hours.* New York: Alfred A. Knopf, 1942.

Weglyn, Michi. *Years of Infamy: The Untold Story of America's Concentration Camps.* New York: William Morrow, 1976.

Wenkham, Robert. *Honolulu Is an Island.* Chicago: Rand McNally, 1978.

NEWSPAPERS AND MAGAZINES

Aberdeen (South Dakota) *American News*
Air Classics magazine
Aerospace Historian
Atlantic Flyer
Chicago Tribune
Denver Post
Edmonds (Washington) *Tribune-Review*
Houlton (Maine) *Pioneer Times*
Life magazine
New Orleans Times-Picayune
New York Times
Oklahoma City Daily Oklahoman
Popular Mechanics magazine
Providence Sunday Journal

Sacramento Bee
San Diego Union
Wall Street Journal
Washington Post

COLLECTIONS

The Milo Ryan Collection of CBS-Radio tapes at the University of Washington, Seattle.

An article by General Roger B. Colton published in *Proceedings of the Institute of Radio Engineers* (November 1945), from the collection of John J. Slattery.

REQUESTS FOR FIRSTHAND ACCOUNTS

The following publications and persons helped with the research for this book by publishing my request for people to tell me their experiences on December 7, 1941.

Los Angeles Times, Washington Post, New York Times, Boston Herald, Ken McClure of *Arizona Senior World,* Jerry Goodrum of *California Senior World,* Jean Godden of *Seattle Post-Intelligencer, Denver Post, Buffalo News,* Ed Hutshing of *San Diego Union,* Patricia Holt of *San Francisco Herald-Examiner, Providence Journal, Dallas Morning News, Arkansas Gazette,* and *Honolulu Advertiser.*

INDIVIDUALS

The following persons, many of whom read of my project in the publications listed above, wrote letters to me with useful information or gave me interviews, or their information was relayed to me by someone else. If I have forgotten anyone, which is almost inevitable with so many people involved, please accept my apologies.

Luke Argilla, D. E. Backinger, Sarah R. Barnes, Vineta D. Bartlett, George M. Baude, Alexander K. Beck, Paul M. Beigelman, John Bladen, Richard Boerner, Jesse Bowman, Marjorie Britt, Marion M. Brown, Madeline Burns, Lois Butler, Maurice W. Carlson, Chet Carsten, Colonel Florence Casey, Frederick W. Chou, Joseph D. Ciparick, Jack Claven, Helen Cobb, Arthur C. Collins, Alan G. Conger, George Constable, James Cox, Robert L. Corbin, M. L. Crawford, Alfred E. Crehan, Gary Curtis.

Antonia Dailey, Julian Davidson, Edgar F. Dickson, Jr., Phyllis Dirks, C. H. Dorsk, Sunni Eckhardt, Alex Edelstein, Henry S. Evans, Dorothy H. Facer, Earl Faith, J. L. Faust, Maurice Featherman, Helen Fefferman, Joel I. Feinberg, Donald A. Field, Doug Fletcher of the *Houlton* (Maine) *Pioneer Times,* Donald E. Forrer, Jane B. Foster, Paul A. Fraser, Selma Gallo, John Garcia, Dan Gerogakas, Mary V. Gillis, Lee A. Gilman, Jean Godden, Cliff Goodall, Benjamin J. Goodman, Richard E. Goodman, Robert H. Gorman, Charles Graham, Jean B. Gregg, Joseph A. Groden.

Jack Hedgecock, Catherine Henderson, R. M. "Mike" Hettema, Walter S. Hochner, Hazel A. Holmann, Franklin W. Hooper, Darrell Illian Hostetter, Betty Huck, Bob Hudson, William R. Hunt, Carl Illian, Mrs. Lawrence J. Jacobs, Mrs. B. B. Johnze, Robert T. Jones, Ilene S. Katz, Larry Katz, Charles W. Kay, Harold S. Kaye, Lysander Kemp, George M. Kerdus, Walter F. Kerrigan, N. Kersnowski, Robert E. Knudson, Karl B. Knust, Audrey Strauss Koch, Herman Koretzky, Hal Kosut.

Tuck Lawlor, Arnold P. Libby, Mrs. Roy V. Lockwood, Robert Loevinger, Thomas A. Lombardi, Arline Jolles Lotman, Louis Lowy, Jack J. Luscher, Robert E. Machol, Lois Malone, Virginia Perkins Mason, Vivian C. Mathews, Robert McAfee, Jr., Dick McBride, Tressa and Bill McCarty, Dr. and Mrs. George R. McCulloch, Paul McCurdy, F. H. McKinstry, Verna M. McMahon, Bob Meek, Morton J. Merowitz, Anne Michaels, Irene Miller, J. R. Miller, Thomas W. Miller, Bart Mills, Robert L. Morris, Leon M. Mosner, E. J. Mowry, C. S. Newcombe, Marian Nilson, James V. Noble, Genevieve G. Oliphant, Barbara W. Olson, Eloise Paananen, Bob Paradise, Nestor Olavi Perala, Marlene Peterson, Olga S. Pottker, Ralph E. Pottker, Russ Potts, Lillian L. Quient, John W. Quinlan.

Henry J. Racette, Robert C. Ramsay, Annice Reskin, Don Rice, Jerome Richard, Wanda Gibson Richardson, Hardee Rives, Armandi Robinson, Mrs. F. F. Robinson, Bonnie Rockhill, Kendra Rogers, Vivian J. Rohrl, Mrs. Warren Rohsenow, R. Ryan, Lenore Sagor, Neil Satterfield, Wayne Satterfield, Clifford L. Sayre, Jr., Lindsley Schepmoes, Albert Schoenfield, Dan R. Schreiner, Mr. and Mrs. William F. Scott, Bill Seril, Ed Sheehan, John J. Slattery, Jane K. Smith, Reverend William A. Spurrier, J. R. Stern, Moneta M. Stewart, Selma H. Stone, Goldie M. Stout, Mary Lou Strachan, Dorothy J. Strum, Edward Stuntz, Edward T. Taveres, Teresa Thomas, Lee Barnwell Thomassen, Lee Thompson, Linore Tiffany, Mrs. Fay Tobias, Walter N. Trenerry, Elinor E. Ulman, Ruth Hill Useem, Mrs. C. G. VanCott, Frank Waldrop, Jack Watson, Edwin A. Weber, Oree C. Weller, Robert Wenkham, Jean West, Elwood L. Whatley, John R. Whiting, Stanley Willis, Don Wilson, Harry Wilson, Carol Jean Wolcott, Marcia Jacobs Wollman, Emily Wong, Gene Woodwick, Mary St. John Zemach.

I am also grateful to Dan Starrer of New York for his help as a researcher in the early stages of this book; to the librarians at the Main Branch of the Seattle Public Library for the enthusiasm and courtesy I learned to take for granted; and to Dan Martinez, historian at the USS Arizona Memorial in Pearl Harbor, Bob Bone, Rich Carroll, Alan Caruba, Jan Graves, Frank Ogden, James Simmons, and Wayne Thoms for suggestions and referrals.

Index

Act of April 16, 1918, 155
Africa, airline service to, 14
airplanes: across Canadian border, 17; construction of, 16
alert systems, 20
Alexander family, 67
Allen, Fred, 6–7
Allen, Gwenfread, 158
Amberg, Julius H., 128
America First, 124–25
American Bureau for Medical Aid to China, 9
American Committee for Nonparticipation in Japanese Aggression, 13
American Legion, 81
Antares, 22–23
antiaircraft batteries, 28, 47, 61, 64, 158
Anzac Clipper, 86–87
Appointment for Love, 6
Arizona, 27, 29, 35, 45, 75
Army: Hawaii preparation, 20; martial law and, 79; numbers in, 102
Army pilots, fighting back at Pearl Harbor, 28
Army Radio Position Finding system. *See* radar
Arnold, Henry "Hap," 94, 96
Asaka, Prince, 12
Associated Press, 112, 122, 133–34
automobiles, 1941 purchases of, 5

Bailey, Joseph F., 8
Baldwin family, 67
Batista, Fulgencio, 104
Battle of Britain, radar used in, 2
"Battle of the Dredge," 37
Bearn, 17
Beck, Alexander K., 62–63
Belin, F. Lammot, 117
Bellows Field, 27
Benny, Jack, 6–7
Bergamini, David, 10
Bergen, Edgar, 6
birth rate, 1930s, 4
Bladen, John, 151–52
blood donors, 77–78
Boerner, Richard, 88–89
Bond, William L., 89
Book, Ann, 149–50

Book, Milton, 149–50
Bremerton, Washington, 139–40
Brereton, Lewis, 94
Britain, assistance to, 16, 17
Brown, Constantine, 102–3
Brown, Kendra Jane, 150–51
Brown, Marion M., 32
Brown, Wilbur, 163
Byas, Hugh, 126

cab drivers, 30
California, 27, 35, 75
California, migration to, 4
Canadian units, Americans serving in, 16
Capetown Clipper, 14–15
Carsten, Chet, 50, 52
Cartwright, Lois, 72
Cassin, 19, 75
Castle, Vernon, 124, 125
Castle family, 67
Caught in the Draft, 6
censorship, 154–55, 160–61
Chiang Kai-shek, 9
Chicago Sun Times, 132
children, effect of Pearl Harbor attack on, 135–41
Childs, John J., 147–48
China: Japan's invasion of, 9; "Tanaka Memorial" version, 10–11
Chinese Americans, 66–69, 109
Chou, Frederick W., 66–69
Christmas leave, 99
Churchill, W., 122
Citizen Kane, 5–6
Civilian Conservation Corps, 100
civilians: casualties, 64; firefighters, 61–63; reactions to war, 161
Clark Field, Philippines, 95–96
classical music, 7
clippers, 14–15, 86–92
Close, Upton, 152
Cobb, Helen, 146
Cobb, Marvin, 146
Coconut Island, 36–37
code machines, 118
comedians, 6–7
Condor, 22
Conger, Alan, 53–57
Cooke family, 67
Corey, H. G. "Steve," 46–48
Costa Rica, response to Pearl Harbor, 129
cotton picker, 4
Cuba, response to Pearl Harbor, 129
Curtiss planes, 17
Curtiss-Wright plant, 100

Daily Oklahoman, 103–4
Daly, John Charles, 101
Davidson, Julian, 142
dead, burying, 30
defense industry, 100; China and, 5; employment in, 8; European allies and, 5
Dirks, Phyllis, 140–41
Dive Bomber, 6
Dole family, 67
Donahue, Harold, 30
Doughty, Hartwell W., 23
Downes, 19, 75
droughts, 3, 4
Dust Bowl, 3

Early, Stephen, 112, 122, 154
East Coast, defending, 162–65
economy, winter of 1941–42, 5
Edwards, Web, 74
Elliott, George, 43–44, 106
Ellis, Steve, 107
employment: defense industry, 8; 1941, 99–100
Enterprise, 2, 87, 159
Evans, Henry S., 2, 9–11, 12–13

farming, mechanized, 3–4
Farm Security Administration, 4
Featherman, Maurice, 34–36
Federal Emergency Relief Administration, 4
Filipino Americans, 109
film industry, 5–6
Finland, England's declaration of war against, 101–2
firefighters, 61–63
Fleming, Robert J., 119
Floyd Bennett Field, 144
Folliard, Edward T., 103
Ford, Robert, 89–92
Ford Island, 3, 56, 159
Forrer, Donald E., 107–8
Fort Monmouth, New Jersey, 2, 162–63
Fort Shafter, 118–19
France: airplanes to, 17; Vichy puppet regime, 18
Fraser, Paul A., 160
friendly fire, 61–65, 159, 160
Fuchida, Mitsuo, 83
Fuchikami, Tadao, 118–19

Garcia, John, 41–42
Germans, in custody after attack, 79
Germany: Japan's pact with, 117; rumors of East Coast invasion, 163
Godden, Jean, 107
Goepner, Oscar W., 22, 23
Golden Gate Bridge, 156
Goodman, Benjamin J., 165
Goodman, Richard, 165
Gordon, John B., 124–25
Gorman, Robert H., 23, 26
Great Britain. *See* Britain
Great Depression, 3, 5
Greenslade, John W., 18
Greevey, Clark, 22
Griffith Stadium, Washington, D.C., 111
Groden, Joseph A., 44–46, 47
Grumman Aircraft, 138
Grumman Wildcats, 87
Guam, Japanese attack on, 93, 123

Hackmeister, Louise, 112
Halifax, Viscount, 122
Hamilton, John, 87–89
Harada, Yoshio, 83–85
Hawaii: military readiness, 19; military taking over, 77–81; radar installed in, 2, 162, 163; radio contact with, 118; tourism, 14. *See also* Honolulu; Pearl Harbor
Hawaiian Airlines, 14–15
"Hawaii Calls," 74
Hawaii Island, 81
health status, 5
Hearst, William Randolph, 6
Hebel, Fritz, 159
Hedgecock, Jack, 51
Helena, 75
Helm, 46
Henderson, Catherine, 149
Henley, 3, 21, 43, 159–60
Hickam Field, 27, 31, 37–41, 62
Hill, L. T., 98
Hirohito, Emperor, 10, 117
Hochner, Walter S., 143–44
Holman, Hazel Amberg, 128
Hong Kong, Japanese attack on, 93, 123
Hong Kong Clipper, 86, 87, 89
Hong Kong Harbor, 89
Honolulu: emergency agencies in, 157; friendly fire in, 61–65; police in, 157–58
Honolulu Advertiser, 68, 70
Honolulu Fire Department, 61–63
Honolulu police force, 49–52
Hooper, Franklin W., 133–34
Hopkins, Harry L., 115–16, 116
Horan, John, 94

Houlton, Maine, 17
Hubbel, Dick, 49, 50, 51
Hull, Cordell, 13, 116, 117, 118
Hungary, England's declaration of war against, 101–2
Hurtsky, J. A., 88

Iceland, 2
Ickes, Harold L., 79–80
Illian, Carl, 32–34
Immigration Station, 79
Indochina, Japan's occupation of, 9
Institute of Pacific Relations, 125–26
International News Service, 112, 122
iron, Japanese purchases of, 8–9, 12, 13
isolationist movement, 9, 12, 13, 125
Italians, in custody after attack, 79
Italy, Japan's pact with, 117
Ito, Kenzo, 156

Japan: America's policy toward, 9; industrial buildup, 8; iron purchases, 8–9, 12, 13; Niihau and, 83; oil supplies, 117; paratroopers, 160; Philippines attack, 93, 94–96; steel industry and, 2
Japanese, in custody after attack, 79
Japanese Americans, 109–10, 152, 156
Japanese consulates, 127–28, 155–56
Japanese Embassy, 117, 127, 155

Kahuku Point, 43
Kaleohano, Hawila, 83–85
Kalimahuluhulu, Kaahakila, 84
Kaltenborn, H. V., 10
Kanahele, Benehakaka, 84–85
Kaneohe Bay, 36
Kaneohe Naval Air Station, 27
Katz, Ilene, 149–50
Katz, Larry, 30
Kay, Charles W., 164–65
Kaye, Harold S., 37–41
Kelley, Gordon L., 38, 40
Kennedy, John F., 111
Kenny, Elizabeth, 5
Kimmel, Husband E., 19, 20, 24, 29, 114, 119
Knox, Frank, 102, 108, 114–15, 120
Kosut, Hal, 107
Kurusu, Saburo, 116–17, 120

labor shortage, 100
Laihana Roads, 19
Latin America: Axis and, 104; response to Pearl Harbor, 129
Lawlor, Tuck, 130
Leahi Home, 78
Leopold III, King, 101
Lewis, Fulton, Jr., 152
Lexington, 2
Lockard, Joseph, 43–44
Lombardi, Thomas A., 28–29

MacArthur, Douglas, 94–95, 96
machine gun nests, 36, 41
Machol, Robert E., 144–45
Magee, John, 11, 12
Malone, Lois, 72
Manchuria, 10, 11
Manhattan Arrows, 111
Manville, Thomas Franklyn, Jr., 98
Marshall, George C., 94, 118, 121
martial law, 77–81, 158
Martinique, supplies to, 18
Maskzawitz, W. C., 24
Matson ships, 14
Mayer, Ferdinand L., 116–17
McCloy, R. C., 22
McCulloch, George, 110
McCulloch, Jean, 110
McCurdy, Paul, 109–10
McLaughlin, Irene Castle, 124, 125
mechanization, displacement of rural people and, 4
Mexico, Tampico harbor, 104

Midway, 88–89, 123
Midwest, migration to, 3–4
military: buildup of, 5; physical standards and, 100; public's attitude toward, 142
military warning network, 163
Miller, Al, 150
Miller, Irene, 150
Mitchell Field, 142–43
Mongolia, 11
movie theaters, 106
Murrow, Edward R., 166–67

Nagy, Robert, 124–25
Nanking, Japanese invasion of, 11–12
naval bases, 102
Navy, reenlistments and, 19–20
Nazis, courting American leaders, 9–10
NBC, 105
Neutrality Act of 1935, 16
Nevada, 21, 27, 31–32, 75
New Caledonia, 90
newspapers, 99, 100, 132–34
news reports, 105–6; censorship and, 154–55
New York Harbor, 162
Niihau Island, 82–85
Nomura, Kichisaburo, 116–18, 120–21
North Africa, Allied forces in, 18
Nye, Gerald P., 124–25

O'Brien, Pat, 111
Office of CIvil Defense, 78
Oglala, 35, 75
Okies, 4
Oklahoma, 27, 35, 75
Oklahoma City, 99
Olson, Barbara, 149
Olson, Orville, 149
Orientals, in Hawaii, 66. *See also* Chinese Americans; Japanese Americans
Outerbridge, William W., 21–22, 23, 25–26

Pacific Clipper, 86, 89–92
Pacific Club, 67
Pacific Fleet, 2–3
Panama Canal, 2
Pan American, 14–15, 86, 107–8
Paradise, Bob, 95
paratroopers, 36
Park, Kay, 103–4
Patterson, Robert, 128
Pearl Harbor: fighting back and, 27–42; first shot, 21–26; predictable operations in, 20; submarines in, 22–24; as a trap, 19
Pearson, Drew, 8
Pennsylvania, 19, 27, 28, 32, 41–42, 75, 159
Peterson, Marlene, 73–74
Philadelphia Eagles, 111
Philippine Clipper, 86, 87–89
Philippines: Japanese attack on, 93, 94–96, 123; radar in, 2
Phoenix, 30, 151
Phoenix, Arizona, Japanese Americans in, 109
Poindexter, Joseph B. 78–80, 123
police, in Honolulu, 157–58
polio victims, 5
Popular Mechanics, 5
Potter, Phil, 166
Pottker, Olga, 151
Pottker, Ralph, 29–30, 151
Powell, Carroll A. "Cappy," 119
Punchbowl Crater, 67

Queen's Hospital, 78
Quinlan, John W., 147

radar: Opana station, 43; Twin Lights station, 162–63; U.S. development of, 1–2

radio: golden age, 6; networks, 112; news, 152; silencing, 77, 80, 160–61
Raenbig, H. W., 23
Ramsay, Robert, 144
recruiting offices, 162
Red Cross, 157
reporters, 133
Rhee, Syngman, 10, 11
Richardson, James, 19–20
Robinson, Aylmer, 84
Robinson family plantation, 82
Roosevelt, Franklin Delano, 79, 166; Hopkins friendship, 115; prewar period and, 16–17; war announcement and, 121–23
Ross, Donald K., 21
Rossi, Angelo J., 156
rumors, unfounded, 158–59, 160–61, 163
Russia, attack on Finland, 102
Ryti, Risto, 101–2

Saikaijo, Shigenori, 83–85
Salvation Army, 157
San Diego, Japanese Americans in, 109
Sand Island, 28
San Francisco, Orientals in, 156
San Jose State College, 49–52
Sato, Yuki, 128
Schoenfield, Albert, 143
Schofield Barracks, 160
seaplane base, 36
Sergeant York, 6, 106
Seril, Bill, 143
servicemen, public's attitude toward, 142
Sevareid, Eric, 166–67
Sharkay, Al, 74–75
Shaw, 75
Sheehan, Ed, 13–14, 18–19, 74–76
shelling, downtown Honolulu, 61
Sherwood, Robert, 115
Shintani, Ishimatsu, 83, 84
Short, Walter C., 20, 78–79, 118, 119, 154
silk trade, 9
Slattery, John J., 1–2, 162–63
Smith, Robert Hall, 46–48
Soloff, George, 30
Sprague, Charles A., 130–31
Spurrier, William A., 111
steel industry, 2, 8, 12, 13
Stewart, Moneta, 150
Stimson, Henry L., 121
Stimson committee, 13
St. John, Harold, 53–54
St. John, Mary, 54, 57–60
stock market crash, 3
Strum, Dorothy, 136
Stuntz, Edward, 129
submarines: attack on Midway Island, 88–89; in Pearl Harbor, 22–24
Sun Valley Serenade, 6
Surles, Alexander D., 154

Tanaka Gi-ichi, 10
"Tanaka Memorial, The," 10
Tanner, William, 22
telephone service, 106–7
Tennessee, 27, 75
Thomassen, Lee Barnwell, 73
Thurston family, 67
Tiffany, Linore, 70–71
Time magazine, 133–34
training films, 146
Trenerry, Walter, 146–47
Trever, 48
Tripartite Pact, 117
Trippe, Juan, 14–16, 108
troop movements, 155
Turner, H. Lanier, 86–87
Turner, Louis P., 38
Twin Lights, 162–63
Two Ocean program, 102
Tyler, Kermit, 43–44

unemployment, 5
unification, 154–56
United Press, 112, 122
University of Hawaii, 49–52
University of Oklahoma, 103–4
Useem, John, 136–39
Useem, Ruth Hill, 136–37
Utah, 45

VanCott, Marjorie, 135

Wake Island, 15, 87, 89, 93, 123
Waldrop, Frank, 111
Ward, 21
Warner, Albert, 101
warship construction program, 16
Washington Redskins, 111
Washington Times Herald, 111–12
Watson, Jack, 129–30
Watson, Paul, 163
Weber, Edwin A., 71–72, 163–64
Welles, Orson, 5–6, 129
Welles, Sumner, 121–22
Wenkham, Robert, 63–65
West Coast, rumors of invasion, 163
Western Union, Marshall's message via, 118
West Virginia, 27, 28, 34, 42, 75
Whatley, Elwood L., 36–37
Wheeler Field, 27, 53–54, 72
White House, preparing for war, 120–23
white supremacy, 67
Whiting, John R., 126–27
Wilkins, Ford, 101
Willamette University, 49–52
Wilson, Don, 3, 44–45, 47, 159–60
Wollman, Marcia Jacobs, 137–38
women volunteers, 161
Wong, Jimmy, 80–81, 157
Wood, Hunter, 21
Woodstock, New Brunswick, 17
Woodward, Clark H., 103
Works Progress Administration (WPA), 100–101, 116

Young, James R., 126
Young, Richard L., 62

ABOUT THE AUTHOR

ARCHIE SATTERFIELD is the author of more than twenty books on history and travel, including *The Home Front: An Oral History of the War Years in America, 1941–1945* (1981). He also writes magazine and newspaper articles on travel, history, and personalities.